"It's a joy to help alleviate pain. It's equally frustrating to see a patient return with chronic pain that was at best temporarily eased. *The Mystery of Pain* puts those cases in context, providing an excellent framework for both patients and health care providers to understand why what works for one may not work for another. Douglas' use of current research and familiar examples clearly explain the revolutionary changes influencing our approach to a growing problem. I highly recommend it for anyone suffering from or treating pain."

—*Celia Bucci MA, LMT, author of* Condition-Specific Massage Therapy

"Douglas Nelson's book *The Mystery of Pain* is a compassionate work from the heart, very important for anyone who wishes to understand healing and to be healed. In this book, we are assisted with deep empathy to open doors to explore this mystery of pain in multiple dimensions. It's a lifelong journey to acknowledge this awareness, one of the universal noble truths we must learn to embrace. Thank you, Douglas, for your compassionate and learned guidance."

—*Chungliang Al Huang, founder-president of the Living Tao Foundation and author of* Embrace Tiger, Return to Mountain: The Essence of Tai Ji

D0921346

of related interest

Principles of Chinese Medicine
Angela Hicks
ISBN 978 1 84819 130 3
eISBN 978 0 85701 107 7

Principles of Reiki
Kajsa Krishni Boräng
Foreword by Wanja Twan
ISBN 978 1 84819 138 9
eISBN 978 0 85701 109 1

Principles of the Alexander Technique
Jeremy Chance
ISBN 978 1 84819 128 0
eISBN 978 0 85701 105 3

Principles of Reflexology
Nicola Hall
ISBN 978 1 84819 137 2
eISBN 978 0 85701 108 4

Principles of Hypnotherapy
Vera Peiffer
ISBN 978 1 84819 126 6
eISBN 978 0 85701 102 2

THE MYSTERY OF PAIN

Douglas Nelson

SINGING
DRAGON
LONDON AND PHILADELPHIA

First published in 2013
by Singing Dragon
an imprint of Jessica Kingsley Publishers
116 Pentonville Road
London N1 9JB, UK
and
400 Market Street, Suite 400
Philadelphia, PA 19106, USA

www.singingdragon.com

Library of Congress Cataloging in Publication Data
Nelson, Andrew, 1978-
  Foundation role plays for autism : role plays for working with individuals with autism spectrum disorders, parents, peers, teachers, and other professionals / Andrew Nelson.
       p. ; cm.
  Includes bibliographical references.
  ISBN 978-1-84905-063-0 (alk. paper)
  1. Autism spectrum disorders--Treatment. 2. Autistic children. 3. Role playing in children--Therapeutic use. I. Title.
  [DNLM: 1. Autistic Disorder--therapy. 2. Adolescent. 3. Child. 4. Role Playing. WS 350.6 N424f 2010]
  RJ506.A9N435 2010
  618.92'891523--dc22
                                    2009039782

British Library Cataloguing in Publication Data
A CIP catalogue record for this book is available from the British Library

ISBN 978 1 84819 152 5
eISBN 978 0 85701 116 9

Printed and bound in Great Britain

*For my wife Janet, whose constant support
helps me to bring ideas to reality.*

CONTENTS

ACKNOWLEDGMENTS. 9

PREFACE: UNDERSTANDING THAT I DON'T UNDERSTAND
The power is in the seeking, not the cup 11

1 A Deeper Understanding of Pain
   Pain as punishment? Seriously?. 17

2 Alarms, Fires, and Alarms without Fires
   Acute vs. chronic pain 23

3 That Which Can Be Known, But Not Often Seen
   Measuring pain. 33

4 Nocere and the Anatomy of Pain
   An early warning defense system. 42

5 When the System Goes Awry
   Peripheral and central sensitization 51

6 The Importance of Meaning and Context
   The stories we tell ourselves. 65

7 Attention and Pain
   Gorilla? What gorilla? 80

8 Fear and Pain
   Be afraid. Be very afraid of being afraid 103

9 Placebos and the Placebo Effect
   I believe, therefore I heal 135

10 Phantom Limb Pain
You don't have to have a leg to have leg pain 146

11 Trigger Points and Referred Pain
An action over here, an effect over there... 155

12 Fibromyalgia
The mystery of pain's poster child 175

13 Social Support and Pain
I am not alone... 187

14 The Pendulum
Now we know what causes <fill in the blank> 198

REFERENCES 208

RECOMMENDED READING 214

INDEX 217

ACKNOWLEDGMENTS

Many people have helped me along the way to realize the dream that became this book. To all of the people who attended my early lectures on this subject, thank you for constantly asking for more to explore, which gave me the idea to turn the lecture into a book.

I wish to especially thank Carol Leseure for the initial reading and editing of the chapters. I am forever grateful for all your help and guidance. Special thanks are also due to Carolyn Mullally, Brenda Nielsen, Brenda Berg, Natalie Frankenberg, and Leslie Mason who read selected chapters and provided feedback. Thank you for giving me honest and helpful critiques. I also wish to thank Dr. Neal Cohen, Dr. Gene Robinson, Dr. Lillian Hoddeson, Dr. Mike Ross, and Dr. Robin McFarquhar for their guidance and inspiration. Thank you also to Chungliang Al Huang for inspiration and a cherished friendship.

I also wish to thank Allison Walker of Jessica Kingsley Publishers for her thoughtful guidance throughout the process of bringing this book to fruition. Thank you for making the process such a wonderful journey.

Lastly, to all the people I have met who, even while experiencing pain, have courageously and consistently continued their daily activities; you were my inspiration for continuing this project.

PREFACE: UNDERSTANDING THAT I DON'T UNDERSTAND

The power is in the seeking, not the cup

I have been treating people with musculoskeletal pain since 1977. Since I treat people who hurt, the most basic skill and knowledge set I should possess is an understanding of what *pain* actually is. I am not sure when this realization hit me, but I came to understand that I did not, at a very deep level, know what pain was, why it happened, and how to treat it effectively. I had focused on the treatment of various conditions such as low back pain, headaches, plantar fasciitis (inflammation of the connective tissue on the sole of the foot), etc. without a deeper understanding of the mechanisms of pain behind the symptom presentation. Needless to say, this realization was humbling. The common denominator of all of the people who sought my help was pain, yet my assumptions about the subject were based on what I had been taught many years ago. Much of what I observed and heard from my clients did not make sense if I evaluated them on the basis of my understanding of pain at that time. Since these clients were clearly sincere and seemed honest about their experiences, I was at a loss to explain the process.

My newfound search for understanding the mystery of pain was exciting and opened a whole new vista in my professional life. Not surprisingly, the pursuit of a deeper understanding of pain made me reassess my assumptions; always the first step in learning is to realize how little one knows at present.

Diving deeply into any subject often produces surprising outcomes, one of the most satisfying aspects of any pursuit of knowledge. Perhaps the outcome that surprised me the most was how my understanding of pain changed the way I practiced my profession. I never thought the study of pain would have such far-reaching practical clinical applications. What began as intellectual curiosity turned into something very applicable.

The more I learn about pain, the more mysteries are unveiled in the process. For every question answered, new questions surface. For all the unanswered questions that still exist, the clinical application keeps evolving and improving. This has been and continues to be enormously gratifying. My hope in writing this book is to share with you the insights of that search and deepen your understanding of the mystery of pain. This should have immediate applications in your personal and professional life.

A constant struggle in writing this book was navigating between two potential downfalls: complexity and over-simplification. A look at the popular press reveals numerous books with a very simplistic approach to pain or that tout a specific methodology of relieving pain. The "Four Easy Steps to Solving All Pain Known to Man" approach is all too common in the popular literature. If there are so many easy solutions readily available, why do we still suffer?

Growing tired of the popular press approach to pain, I began to delve into the current scientific literature to understand pain more deeply. What I found was more interesting than I could have ever imagined. Pain research is one of the most exciting frontiers of science and the story is continuously unfolding.

Realistically, however, the academic literature is not immediately accessible to the general population. Many scientists are immersed in their area of interest but can't really relate what they are studying to the rest of us. Admittedly, that isn't their job. The shadow side of this myopia is that the general public often finds the research to be complicated and of little relevance to daily life. The science is complex, but it reveals numerous windows of opportunities to positively affect our experiences of pain, especially chronic pain. If you or your loved ones suffer from chronic pain, my hope is to enlighten you to the emerging science and show you possible strategies to combat pain, based on a new and deeper understanding.

An omission in this book is the area of pharmacology and pain. I have not included information on the role of medication and pain control because there is a plethora of good books on the subject. The reader will have very little trouble finding excellent and credible information.

Why the title *The Mystery of Pain*? One of my favorite writers, Malcolm Gladwell, wrote a wonderful piece on the difference between a mystery and a puzzle. In a puzzle, one missing piece is all you need to complete the process. You struggle because you don't have something you need. In a mystery, what you need is a deeper understanding, perhaps just a different interpretation, of what is already in front of you. As the saying goes, "When trying to find a needle in a haystack, more hay won't help."

The process of pain is very much a mystery rather than a puzzle. For years, I operated from the older model of pain which I had learned previously and simply ignored the aspects of pain that conflicted with that viewpoint. Only when I started to question the structure of my understanding did the real fallacy of my assumptions become obvious. The old model viewed chronic pain with much the same lens as it did acute pain. The old model assumed that pain is a messenger warning us of possible damage, and the amount of pain experienced is in linear proportion to the severity of the pathology that caused it. The new science reveals that in the case of chronic pain, the *messenger* is the problem. Chronic pain can also be completely non-linear; debilitating pain can be present with no obvious source while very serious pathologies may present with no pain at all.

Given the very nature of pain, it is no wonder how complicated and confusing the subject can be. Pain can be as simple as pulling your hand away from something sharp and as complex as Post-Traumatic Stress Disorder (PTSD) or phantom limb pain. With complexity comes the potential to misinterpret data, leading us down completely errant paths. Unfortunately, for the pain sufferer, this makes a bad situation much worse.

The old model also suggested that pain is a response to an offense, from which it then follows that people who are in pain must have done something to cause the suffering. If emotions affect pain, then perhaps one's negative emotions are the source of the pain in the first place. Essentially, you hurt because of the way you think and interpret the world. On a purely physical level, if movements cause pain, then movement should be avoided.

These types of thinking are understandable, yet misguided and potentially very damaging. They come from a misinterpretation of the process of pain using old and no longer valid ways of understanding. How do we move beyond this model to a new interpretation of pain? A deep exploration of the current science of pain will facilitate this transition.

As we make that transition, it is important not to lock on to any of this as an absolute—thus replacing an old, rigid model with a new one, just as rigid. Understanding is an evolving process, one that happens in layers.

As we explore the mystery of pain, you will discover that the process of pain in the human body is amazingly complex. While one would assume that the physical aspects of the process of pain are rather straightforward, this turns out not to be true. Correct signals can be magnified out of proportion. Incorrect signals can be sent. Nerve receptors switch jobs and over-respond. In some ways, it is like crowd behavior gone bad. In the end, everyone feels justified in yelling, but no one is exactly sure what they are yelling about. The sensitivity and complexity of the nervous system can veer wildly off course and the end result is a body in pain.

The experience of pain also entails numerous ways in which the psychological approach of the sufferer can influence the experience. Beyond the physical level, social and cultural influences have a tremendous impact on the experience of pain. How the brain and psyche interpret the experience of pain can dampen or intensify the experience. Numerous factors can influence your experience of pain in either direction.

If there is one lesson to learn in these pages, that lesson is this: The more deeply you understand the process of pain, the more power you have to influence it. You cannot influence a system that you do not understand. Central to this understanding is that pain is often the summation of multiple factors:

$$\text{Factor A + factor B + factor C + factor D} = P \text{ (pain)}$$

Changing something on the left side of the equation will change the outcome (pain) on the right. If you only desire to change the answer (the right side of the equation where P = Pain) without addressing anything on the left side of the equation, you are in for a long and frustrating experience. Yet, this is indeed what many patients want from their healthcare providers—just stop the pain without making any changes in behavior or experience (the left side of the equation). Unfortunately, medicine has been all too happy to oblige. Whether this is driven by physician attitudes or by patients who push for easy answers, the end result is the same. Ultimately, we must transition to a different and more collaborative way of thinking and dealing with pain.

Another lesson of this book is the elusive nature of pain with regard to diagnosis. Unfortunately, pain cannot be seen via imaging technology and this presents huge challenges for everyone involved. You may be able to see disc pathology on a magnetic resonance imaging (MRI) scan, but that pathology may have nothing to do with the person's pain. Arthritis may be seen on an X-ray, but that does not correlate well to people's experience of pain. What we are left with is simply the patient's self-reporting of being in pain. Patients often think that their doctors do not believe them and therefore feel invalidated. Doctors question the accuracy and validity of the patient's account, not knowing whether to trust the patient or the diagnostic images and lab tests. For many years of medical history, if the pathology could not be seen, then the pain was ascribed to psychological causes or secondary gain (that the patient has somehow benefited from being sick). This led to an adversarial and distrustful relationship between patient and provider.

If you suffer from chronic pain, my hope is to enlighten you as to the process of pain and show you possible strategies based on the emerging science. If you are a family member or friend of someone in pain, this book can help you understand the process of pain more deeply and thus be a more empathetic support system for your loved one.

CHAPTER 1

A DEEPER UNDERSTANDING OF PAIN
Pain as punishment? Seriously?

Pain. Just thinking the word gives most of us a deeply unpleasant response. The concept of pain conjures up images of past experiences of suffering, either emotionally or physically. Pain is the antithesis of pleasure and an experience we generally try to avoid at all costs. It is like the unforgiving exactor of justice, punishing us for a transgression committed. If our own experience isn't bad enough, we can also suffer when witnessing pain in our loved ones. When we hear that someone is dying, we immediately want to know if they are suffering and in pain.

No matter how obvious and simple the experience of pain seems at first, our concepts and models of pain often break down under scrutiny. First of all, are pain and suffering the same thing? Can you have pain and not suffer? If I asked you to recall a time of much pain in your life, some would vividly recall physical pain, while others would remember psychological pain. While different, both are forms of pain. If pain is to be avoided and pleasure is to be sought, how would you explain the pain an athlete willingly suffers in preparation for a marathon or the Tour de France? How would you also explain how the body knows that selected pain is inherently beneficial, such as when a therapist massages sore spots in your shoulders or your spouse removes a splinter you cannot reach? If pain is bad, why are some experiences of pain pleasurable?

Perhaps the most common belief about pain is that pain is the body's response to an offense committed against itself. Consider the foundations of the word itself: the Latin origin of the word pain is *poena*, meaning punishment, vengeance, or penalty. (Curiously, I had never considered the origin of the word *subpoena*.) The model of pain as the exactor of justice starts to break down very quickly under further scrutiny. If we take pain at its simplest level, pain as punishment seems reasonable. When one overdoes alcohol, the headache that comes with a hangover becomes a clear reminder to drink less next time. Pain as punishment seems like justice for a transgression committed.

What, however, are we to make of pain that is not easily relegated to the pain as punishment paradigm? What do we make of the pain of a migraine? For what is the pain punishing the sufferer? Where is the offense? What about pain in a limb that doesn't exist (phantom limb pain)? What about someone, like a friend of mine, who is inconsolable after the death of his wife. He is in serious pain; he is truly suffering. Is his pain a punishment for loving someone so completely and so very deeply? Conversely, when cancer begins to ravage the body, why is there often no pain that accompanies the pathology? If pain is a warning sign, where is the pain when you need it?

Defining pain

If we are going to examine how to influence pain, we must first agree on a definition of what pain is. Here is the academic definition of pain from the International Association for the Study of Pain (IASP) (www.iasp-pain.org):

> An unpleasant sensory and emotional experience associated with actual or potential tissue damage, or described in terms of such damage.

I'll bet I know what you are thinking; probably very similar to what I thought when I read this definition for the first time.

"Who wrote this, a lawyer?" It does resemble the kind of legal mumbo jumbo that ends up meaning nothing of practical value. In truth, though, the more you understand about pain, you will see that this definition is well conceived and reflects the most accurate understanding of pain today.

Let's break the definition down to make more sense of it. First, pain is unpleasant. Earlier in this chapter, I equated pain with suffering. There are scholars who would probably argue that point, which is an understandable debate at a theoretical level. In real life, however, pain and suffering are often very much intertwined.

In the old model, pain was a rather mechanical reaction to a negative stimulus; a completely physical event. Suffering, on the other hand, was an emotional experience. The stark division between these two experiences most likely resides in the concept of the separation of mind and body. Pain is physical, suffering is emotional; both can be independent of the other. It is a convenient way to draw clear lines, but life often has little to do with clear lines.

Over the last few decades, the idea that mind and body are separate has been supplanted by a model in which mind and body are completely intertwined. New fields of study, such as psychoimmunology, have emerged. These new disciplines aren't simply a reaction to a shift in philosophy, they exist in response to new technologies that allow scientists to measure that which could never previously be measured. The physical effects of emotional experiences can now be seen with functional magnetic resonance imaging (fMRI) and a host of other technologies that allow researchers to observe changes in the body and brain, never before measured. Subtle changes in immune function can now be tracked in ways previously unimaginable. Moving from philosophy to fact has been an extreme change, one that medicine is still learning how to integrate into clinical practice.

Notice how the IASP definition of pain states that pain is an unpleasant sensory *and* emotional experience. It does not say sensory *or* emotional experience. If pain was merely physical sensation, then it could be a purely physical response to a defined negative stimulus. Emotions would have nothing to do with it, positively or negatively. Our experience tells us differently.

In fact, emotions and pain are inexorably connected. We will explore later the power of our emotional response to pain. Emotions can either escalate or dampen the experience of pain tremendously. If pain is sensory *and* emotional, then understanding this could be a very useful tool, allowing the process to work for us, not inadvertently working against us. The deeper our understanding of the process of pain, the less we are likely to fear it. And as you will see, fear increases the experience of pain while a sense of control lessens the experience of pain. Knowledge can be powerful medicine.

Notice that the definition also states that the pain experience is associated with actual *or potential* tissue damage. Is the victim about to be tortured in pain even before the abuse begins? Then again, does the abuse have to be physical to be devastating? One of the trademark techniques of torture is that the victim is allowed to meticulously view or hear the objects intended to be used during the torture. Seeing the pliers, the victim imagines what his/her captor is going to do with the instrument. This imagining is already in the category of pain, something that people who torture know very well.

In a more broad application, the pain does not have to come from a "real" or visible source to be valid. There is a truism for those who treat pain which states, "The patient is always in exactly as much pain as they say they are." As you might imagine, this can lead to much difficulty and suspicion for healthcare providers who want to see clear pathology in a diagnostic image that will validate the patient's experience of pain. Lacking that visible evidence can lead to suspicion on the part of the healthcare provider and a feeling of invalidation for the patient. A better understanding of pain would help both patient and physician.

On the patient side, the old understanding of pain can lead to self-doubt about one's own experience. When a physician cannot find a source of the pain you feel, you can either question the health provider or question yourself. If you hurt, there must be a source of the pain, some sort of offense or pathology to which the pain is alerting you. As you will see in the following pages, that isn't always true: pain cannot be seen on a diagnostic image and chronic pain doesn't even need a source to exist. Pain validates itself.

Stating that "pain validates itself" is one thing, but standing firm when medical professionals start to question whether your pain is psychological is quite another. I recently witnessed this situation with one of my clients, a very bright professor who had always been slender and extremely active. About ten years ago, she had an episode where she felt terrible for several weeks and then began to experience very uncomfortable generalized pain. She began to gain weight at a surprising rate, even though her diet was well controlled. The source of her musculoskeletal pain was not clear, but it severely hampered her activity level. As a result, she limited her caloric intake even further. This had no effect on her weight, which kept climbing. When I saw her, she was by no means severely overweight, but certainly not the slender woman of her recent past.

During her ten-year odyssey with pain, not a single intervention helped her. Nothing could be found in any diagnostic test, yet many guesses as to the nature of her problem were explored and then abandoned. When that didn't help, the emphasis shifted to the "You must be depressed" category, rather than pursuing further efforts to solve the problem. During this whole process, her courage and personal conviction stayed firm. She knew that the problem was real and there must be an answer somewhere. Indeed, she found a very wise physician who diagnosed her correctly (an intestinal inflammation) and the results were absolutely astonishing. While the particulars of her case are interesting, the greater miracle is this woman's courage to hold fast while everyone seemed to doubt her. Her experience is unfortunately not a rarity; her courage is inspiring.

The old model of pain can be just as frustrating for health providers as well. In medical school, students are taught how to solve problems. If a patient presents with pathology, the physician is taught how to diagnose and treat the disease appropriately. Medical education is a triumph of knowledge, and the faculty and medical students I have met are very bright and sincere people.

Unfortunately, many of the patients these young physicians will see after graduation do not fit into such a concise realm of treatment. How do you deal with conditions where the client is suffering and you cannot simply fix it? Furthermore, what about patients like my client? Her problem was solvable, but no doctor she had seen had experience with anything of that nature. Of course, there are patients who do catastrophize pain, but they are certainly in the minority of daily clinical experience. In the old model, pain is a byproduct of pathology. Find and resolve the cause and the pain will disappear. Unfortunately, as you might expect, it often does not work this way. That leaves physicians feeling frustrated and ineffective, and too often patients are pushing for simple answers and quick resolution. If both providers and patients understood the science of pain more deeply, greater trust could mean more effective care. It is my sincere hope that this book can help bridge that gap.

CHAPTER 2

ALARMS, FIRES, AND ALARMS WITHOUT FIRES
Acute vs. chronic pain

The philosopher René Descartes referred to pain as like a rope ringing a bell. When an outer noxious stimulus acts upon the body, the nervous system responds with an appropriate warning message, which is perceived as pain. This model of thinking dominated the understanding of pain for many years and is the essence of the older model of pain referred to earlier. For some types of pain, this model seems perfectly appropriate. For other types of pain, Descartes' rope and bell model doesn't explain what people experience.

As it turns out, there are really two types of pain and they are radically different. One of them follows very specific rules and general patterns and the pain seems like a perfectly appropriate response to prevent further injury. The other type of pain does not fit the rope and bell model in the least. Let's explore each of these types of pain individually.

Acute pain: Fire! No, really!

When most people hear the word pain, they typically think of acute pain. A negative stimulus produces the experience of pain to warn us to discontinue the offending activity. In this case, pain is useful and necessary, potentially even life-saving. Let's explore a few aspects of acute pain to get a deeper understanding:

Pain = Damage (You have been served a warning)

Perhaps the most important aspect of acute pain is that the pain really does warn us of impending damage. If you are holding your neck in an awkward position while fixing something under the kitchen sink, the muscles of your neck may communicate the need to take a break sooner rather than later. Holding the muscles in such an awkward position could create some serious problems if this message went unheeded for an extended period of time.

Pain as a warning of impending damage seems very simple, but it can be complicated by several factors. It is not easy to decide if the pain is something you should heed or not. For instance, I would wager that most of us have had pain during an activity such as strenuous exercise. I would also bet there are times when you just decided to continue exercising and the pain eventually disappeared. I would also assume that there have been times when you should have ceased the activity sooner, as continuing the exercise had negative consequences. Knowing when to push yourself, thus expanding your capabilities, and when to stop because further activity could be dangerous is not an easy decision to make.

There is a theory that has been floating around in sport science for a few years called the Central Governor Theory that sheds light on the brain and exertion. In this theory, the brain uses pain as a message to tell you when to stop exerting yourself. In the theory, the general understanding is that pain will appear before you completely "run out of gas," so that you will stop before you are completely exhausted or injured.

There are many aspects to the Central Governor Theory that are really interesting, but two of them apply directly to our discussion of pain. First, pain is used as a warning sign to cease activity before the onset of serious injury. How do elite athletes confront that pain and push past it, knowing that there is still "gas in the tank"? How does their brain know when to heed the message of pain and when to ignore it to achieve greatness? Second, the theory has taken some heat because the name "Central Governor" implies just that: that there is some central place where all the decisions are made. In reality, no such place can be found. There are multiple systems in the body affected by severe exertion and probably all of them have input into the brain. If you are looking for one central location for a governing mechanism, none has been found so far.

So it is with pain on both counts. When we have acute pain, how is it that we can ignore some pain and generally do well, while we know other kinds of pain really should not be ignored? How do we know the difference? Additionally, where in the brain does pain exist? Like over-exertion affecting multiple systems, pain also seems to affect multiple parts of the brain. Therefore, there is no imaging technique that can point to any one part of the brain as the center of pain.

In the Central Governor Theory, the athlete can decide (cognitively) to override the messages of pain and exhaustion coming from the body. This is a closed system: the athlete is ignoring messages coming from his/her own body. What can complicate the process of cognitive override is an outside influence such as a coach or trainer. If your coach pushes you beyond limits previously thought possible, you discover new horizons in fitness. On the other hand, push too far and the athlete can risk serious injury, such as a high school football player dying while doing practices twice a day in intense heat. A delicate potential negative effect of aggressive coaching is that the athlete learns not to listen to his/her own body, surrendering control to a higher authority. While there is no easy answer to this dilemma, it certainly underscores the need for knowledgeable coaches in children's sport. If control is ceded to others, coaches must know what they are doing based on sound physiological principles and a deep understanding of the process.

Enforced rest

Another role of pain is to force the person to rest after an injury. If you have punctured the bottom of your foot and it is still painful to step on, you will be forced to rest until it is no longer uncomfortable to bear weight. While enforced rest in response to acute pain is necessary, resting a chronic injury is often not helpful at all. In fact, it often makes the problem worse. In problems like tennis elbow, resting it often does nothing to help. Worse yet, the muscles are getting progressively deconditioned from lack of use, which further disposes them to injury when activity is resumed.

The scorecard

If you tear a hamstring, the pain you experience during activity is generally reflective of how the recovery of the muscle is going. In this case, pain acts like a scorecard telling you how much activity you can resume. If you still have a great deal of pain, you can do only very little activity. If you are 80 percent better, you should expect to feel 80 percent less pain. Acute pain is *generally* reflective of severity. A little pain means a small problem, a lot of pain means you'd better get help fast. Unfortunately, as we will discover later, chronic pain does not follow these rules.

The teacher

An often overlooked aspect of pain is its ability to be an educator, helping us to make better choices in future decisions. If every time you over-eat you feel terrible, the pain can serve to influence future behavior. Doing anything to excess can create pain: drinking too much, exercising too much, or being too sedentary. These messages are learning opportunities that we may or may not heed.

We certainly all know people who chose not to heed those early warnings and the end result was disastrous. We often wonder why they did not acknowledge the warning signs earlier and change the offending behavior. While these people may not have heeded the message, the warning sign of pain was certainly present. Pain was trying to teach them; they just did not want to hear the message.

If pain is to be a teacher, the lesson must be heeded and remembered the next time the behavior presents itself. Later in the book, we will explore the ways in which memory and pain are linked.

Source identification and elimination

When pain arrives, the quality, severity, and location can all be clues to the source. More than anything else, the brain needs to know the source of pain. Pain in the foot resulting from plantar fasciitis is very different from having a pebble in your sandal. We don't think much about this, but we know what a pebble in a shoe feels like. Generally, we do not know what a stress fracture in the fifth metatarsal feels like because we don't have a historical experience to draw upon to identify it.

As we go through life, various pains are stored in our memory bank and are linked to corresponding causes. As a result, our first response is to eliminate the cause; if we can, then pain has done its job. In addition, we are far less anxious about known causes of pain than unknown causes. If the cause is unknown, it implies that we cannot eliminate that which we cannot identify. In the end, that may be a much bigger problem than the pain we are experiencing at present.

Seeking comfort

Pain causes us to act, to move to lessen or eliminate the discomfort. In many cases, this alone is of vital importance. There is a phenomenon in physical medicine called an *antialgic position*. *Anti*, meaning against and *algia*, meaning pain. It is your body's defense mechanism against pain, to seek a position where the pain lessens.

Here is one example. Have you ever seen someone with a recent bout of back pain where it looks as if his/her hips are shifted off to one side? In the mechanistic view, the tempting thing to do is to straighten him/her up, to align the hips over the rest of the body. This will prove disastrous as the shifted (asymmetrical) position is the body's way of unloading stress on an inflamed spinal disc. The body knows that standing in a seemingly asymmetrical way is the only position that lessens the pain. This is not to be corrected; it is to be heeded. When the disc is better, posture will also be better. Pain tells us not only that something hurts, but the absence of pain tells us this is a relieving posture, which is equally important.

A life without pain: Not what you'd wish for

In summary, acute pain is pain with a purpose. It is vital to our existence and is a guiding force in shaping behavior that keeps us safe. Inability to experience pain is life-threatening. As an example, there are people who are born without the ability to experience pain, a condition called Congenital Indifference to Pain (CIP). These unfortunate people are normal in other ways (they can sense touch, know where they are in space, etc.), but they do not experience pain. If they fell off a ledge, they would not know if a bone was broken. A serious cut would be unannounced, except for the visual confirmation of blood, which would eventually demand attention. Many of them have their teeth removed at a very early age because they cannot tell if they are biting the tongue. There are cases where children with this condition have rubbed an eye (as children mindlessly do) so frequently that the eye had to be removed.

As you can imagine, the life span of people with CIP is quite limited due to the number of injuries that can go unattended. Many die before the age of three; seldom do any of these people live beyond their early twenties. Thankfully, this disorder is extremely rare. Pain, the nemesis for so many, is also a terrible condition for those for whom it is not present.

In the end, acute pain serves many useful, even life-saving, purposes. The qualities and strategies of acute pain which are so effective in the short term become very problematic when applied in the long term. Processes meant to protect us end up being the cause of much suffering. Thus begins our exploration of chronic pain.

Chronic pain: Fire! At least there was one, I think...

Chronic pain and a faulty alarm system

The bulk of this book explores the experience of chronic pain, which affects as much as 15 percent of the world's population. At its essence, chronic pain is very different from acute pain on many levels. First, let's review the International Association for the Study of Pain definition of chronic pain:

> Pain that outlasts normal healing time or after the noxious stimulius is no longer active.

There are a couple of very important issues inside this definition, which are at the heart of the mystery of pain.

It isn't really about time...

Most of us think of acute pain as short term and chronic pain as long term. In a small way, this is true. The complexity of chronic pain is much deeper than simply time, however. Each injury has a predicted future course of events (prognosis) which is an extremely useful guideline for provider and patient alike. If you cut your foot, you want to know what the timeline for recovery is and what to expect along the way. The same is true with a fracture to a bone: there is a fairly consistent timeline of healing.

29

In chronic pain, the pain exists long after the expected healing time has taken place. To complicate matters further, most often the injury itself seems to have healed, but the pain remains. Your foot may look fine and the scar has healed nicely, but the pain stays with you every step you take.

It is here that the idea of pain as a warning sign begins to break down and the real mystery of pain begins. In our earlier example of a fracture in one of the small bones of the foot, your doctor may see exactly the healing he/she hoped for after six to eight weeks. In cases where a bone was fractured and has healed, the bone repair will be visible on the X-ray. When this repair process is pointed out to you in the office, you may be less than impressed with this information. All you know is regardless of how good the X-ray looks, your foot hurts. The doctor could be a little frustrated at this point, but his/her frustration is no match for how frustrated you may be feeling. Given a visual inspection and the timeline, you should be doing fine. You know you are far from being fine.

When a fractured bone is "healed" but the pain remains, this leads us to the other part of the definition of chronic pain (*or after the noxious stimulus is no longer active*). Imagine a fire alarm announcing flames coming from the kitchen (analogous to acute pain). Now, the flames have been put out, there are no visible signs of fire, but the alarm continues to shriek. At that point, the alarm is just as bad (or worse) than the fire. The deafening sound of the alarm continues to concern you, but you can see no fire. If a fire is present, the alarm is less annoying because you understand the connection between the sound and the visible flames. Perhaps the worst aspect of the constant alarm is that you do not know whether to heed the warning or to ignore it. Is the alarm telling you that there are embers still smoldering that may reignite and take the rest of the house down? Or, can you just disable the alarm system and clean up the mess? With the alarm still going, neighbors are possibly getting worried about their own house being affected and your ability to assure them is limited because you are ultimately unsure about the reality of the situation. Everyone involved gets sensitized because the alarm just won't shut off. This is exactly what happens in chronic pain. The "fire" (injury) doesn't need to exist to keep the alarm (pain) going.

Of what possible evolutionary use is chronic pain

Brenda Nielsen, one of the therapists in my office, first asked this question a few years ago and I was fascinated by it. When you examine so many other aspects of our physiology, there are clear reasons to see how various traits developed over time. Our response to acute pain makes perfect sense and is finely tuned to keep us from harm. While the evolutionary benefit of acute pain can be understood, how could chronic pain be of use to us? From an evolutionary perspective, why wouldn't the traits that make chronic pain possible eventually be selected out over time?

One possible answer goes back to the aforementioned idea that employing short-term responses longer term can have serious consequences. Processes meant to protect us end up harming us. An example of a short-term strategy gone overboard involves neutrophils, a type of white blood cell that marshals your defenses against infection. These little killers are meant to destroy any kind of foreign invader present in a wound. In an interesting twist, any kind of tissue damage, even spraining an ankle, sends neutrophils to the rescue. Think about this: in a sprain, there is no possibility of infection because there is no breach of the skin. Yet, the body sends an army of neutrophils to the rescue, just in case. Mistaking substances released during the injury (such as your own cell mitochondria released during the micro-tearing of tissue) as foreign, the neutrophils start attacking everything in sight. They shoot first and ask questions later. To use our early fire metaphor, they pour water on anything that looks like smoke.

Obviously, this can have dire consequences. Neutrophils can also attack our own cells, mistaking them for invaders. This is the essence of auto-immune disorders. Why hasn't this tendency to over-respond diminished over time? The answer probably lies in the deadly potential of letting the guard down if foreign substances are indeed in the tissue. While the cost of over-sensitivity is great, the cost of diminished sensitivity is far greater. Let one infection go unchecked and the results could be fatal. The safest strategy is to shoot everything that moves, just in case. This tendency is also wired into our brains in other ways. If you walk in the woods and see something that resembles a snake, you react first and think second. Nine times out of ten, this reaction is overkill. That said, the one time you don't jump out of harm's way may have a fatal consequence. Your brain doesn't take that chance; neutrophils don't take that chance. As a result, we suffer more than our share of "friendly fire," especially when it comes to injuries that have no real possibility of infection.

Perhaps the same general process occurs with chronic pain. Pain is known to affect emotional centers of the brain, attention centers, areas involved with movement, memory, decision-making, and much more. All of these brain regions play an important role in protcting us during acute pain. Like the previous example regarding neutrophils, perhaps these protective mechanisms actually become the problem when they are unchecked and out of control. Pain mechaisms meant to protect us from harm end up making life miserable.

CHAPTER 3

THAT WHICH CAN BE KNOWN, BUT NOT OFTEN SEEN
Measuring pain

As mentioned earlier, the presence of pain is not something that can be easily observed on a diagnostic image. If there is no clinically easy way to diagnose pain via a test, then how do doctors measure pain? Just about every person with experience in pain management will grimace when they read this, but the answer is the lowly pain scale. From offices like mine, to physician's offices, to gatherings of the crème de la crème of pain scientists, the pain scale is ubiquitous in assessing how much pain a person is experiencing.

First, I should say something about diagnostic tests and healthcare. If you give blood for a blood panel, no one asks your opinion about your cholesterol level. You can protest that your diet has improved greatly, but your perception about the results of the blood test doesn't carry much weight. The test reveals the facts, unblemished by your version of what you think is occurring. Someone applying for a security position might say he/she never uses illicit drugs, but if cocaine shows up in a urine test, the verbal denial doesn't count for much. People can lie or omit facts; tests don't. As a result, medicine has moved as far as possible to the use of infallible diagnostic testing instead of relying on patient accounts. Doctors don't always trust patients, patients don't always trust doctors. The cold feeling we get when reading the results of our lab report is indicative of this dynamic. You can't study for a blood test; it is what it is. Tests such as this are an unforgiving scorecard for a game in which the rules have often never been explained.

Unlike the cold objective reality of the blood test, the pain scale is totally dependent on what we, the patient, report. Patients often dislike it because they think the scale is simplistic and don't really know how to rate their pain. Doctors dislike it because they don't trust the patient to report accurately. Despite its shortcomings, the pain scale is still the most commonly used tool we have at present to measure pain. Let's explore the scale just a bit more to understand what it is and how it is used.

There are essentially two types:

- *Verbal Reporting Scale (VRS)*. In this scale the patient is typically asked to give the pain a number, either from 1–10 or 1–100 with the lowest number being no pain at all and the highest number being the most difficult pain you have ever had or could imagine.

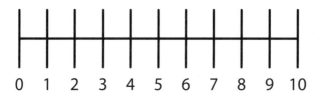

Figure 3.1: Verbal Reporting Scale

- *Visual Analog Scale (VAS)*. In this scale, the person might be shown a line that is ten centimeters in length and asked to mark the severity of pain with 0 being no pain and 10 being the most difficult pain you have ever had or could imagine. In some instances, faces are used to illustrate the scale; this is often used when measuring pain in children.

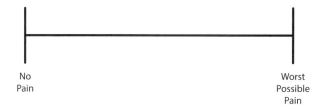

Figure 3.2: Visual Analogue Scale

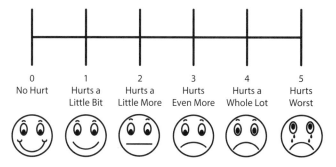

Figure 3.3: Faces Scale

One of the glaring problems with the both of these scales is reference points. The person is told that the highest number is the most difficult pain you have ever had or could imagine. What happens if the person has had relatively little pain in life, no broken bones, no traumas, etc.? How should she/he calibrate the present pain in relationship to a terrible pain never yet experienced? In that case, one can only imagine a serious pain. As many people know, imagining the pain of a kidney stone and actually *having* a kidney stone are not quite the same.

In the reverse, if you have suffered greatly, the pain of a fracture or kidney infection may seem nothing insurmountable. In 1994, I went with some remarkable people on a mission trip to bring healthcare to the indigenous Indians in the mountains of El Salvador. My job each morning was to teach the Salvadorans simple ways to help each other using massage techniques, then treat community members who had muscular pain in the afternoons. These people had suffered unspeakable horrors at the hands of government soldiers in the 1980s, atrocities too terrible to imagine. When I was treating an overworked and strained muscle with my hands, I was intrigued by the response of these remarkable Salvadorans. On my treatment table at home, people commonly react strongly to discomfort produced by my pressure (which is perfectly appropriate). Among Salvadoran people who have suffered so much, having a skinny Norwegian (me) pushing on a sore spot in a muscle doesn't rate very high on the list of unpleasant things they have ever experienced. I can clearly remember how little reaction my pressure elicited from these people: not a wince, a flinch, nothing.

Patient reporting has other complicating factors. Asking a patient to self-assess opens the door to a host of problems that could influence the accuracy of the scale. To explore this, let's review two definitions first, pain threshold and pain tolerance.

- *Pain threshold.* The least experience of pain which a subject can recognize.

- *Pain tolerance.* The greatest level of pain which a subject is prepared to tolerate.

It is common for the general public to use the terms *pain tolerance* and *pain threshold* interchangeably. In truth, they refer to different concepts, except that both refer to the experience of the person in pain. Pain threshold is the minimal amount of a stimulus that is perceived as painful. Researchers often test this with thermal sensations such as extreme heat or cold. For example, a scientist may perform this study having a subject hold an object in his/her hand that gets increasingly hot. Subjects are asked to report when the object gets hot to the point of being uncomfortable. The temperature at which it becomes unpleasant is the pain threshold. Interestingly, if you test the same individual over time, even years later, the pain threshold level does not vary significantly. The variance in temperature reported by subjects is only in the range of 0.2 degrees Celsius, which is remarkably small.

Pain tolerance refers to the amount of discomfort the person will endure before employing strategies to cease the offending stimulus. In classic studies with cold water, typically about 5 degrees Celsius, two subjects may perceive the temperature as uncomfortable, but one may tolerate having an arm immersed in the cold water for much longer than another. As you might imagine, pain tolerance can vary wildly, not only from person to person, but even in the same person at different points, depending on other factors.

As an example, one study by Lynette Dufton and colleagues (2008) explored the effect of stress and pain tolerance in children with recurrent abdominal pain. Using cold water as the test (how long can you keep your hand in 5 degrees Celsius water), the children were given baseline tests to assess their pain tolerance. Then the children were given a stressful task (serial subtraction) and had their pain tolerance tested again. The stress of the subtraction test lowered their pain tolerance, showing that stress can indeed lower pain tolerance in children.

For an extreme example of pain tolerance, I remember an incident relayed to me by a friend of mine who is a certified athletic trainer for a college basketball team. He was once walking off the court with a player, who, out of the blue, mentioned that he might have torn his quadriceps (a very large thigh muscle) two days before. At first, the trainer dismissed the statement, telling the player that if he had torn his quadriceps he would have known it immediately. The player seemed to accept this explanation and the two of them continued walking towards the training room. The more the trainer thought about that comment (and knowing this athlete's pain tolerance was off the charts), the more he wondered if the player could have tolerated such a major injury for two days. Upon investigation, he found that the player had completely torn a section of muscle and had said nothing for two days. That is pain tolerance to the extreme, which can be an asset in the short term and also a potential long-term liability. Ignoring the initial warning signs of pain can potentially lead to far more serious injuries.

Beyond individual variances, let's look at three other factors in pain thresholds and tolerance: gender, culture, and race.

Research shows that there is a small but measurable difference between males and females with regard to pain thresholds and also pain tolerance. Females have a slightly lower pain threshold than do males, meaning that a female will perceive a stimulus as painful before a male will. While this difference is small, it is at least measurable. (This was surprising to me, as I had assumed that a typical female pain tolerance level would be greater than a male's and therefore so would her threshold.)

A number of studies have looked at this effect from both a sex and gender perspective. One's sex is generally a given, but identification with a gender role is quite variable. Some men are more sensitive, which is typically seen as a female trait, while some women identify more with a typically male gender role.

Emily Wise and her colleagues (2002) looked at gender roles and pain. One hundred and forty-eight subjects, 87 males and 61 females, underwent testing of pain tolerance, threshold, and VAS ratings to a very hot probe. To test threshold, the subjects had the probe on the left forearm. When they sensed that the stimulus had reached a painful level, they were to say the word "pain." When the increasingly hot probe had met their tolerance for discomfort, they were to simply say the word "stop."

Women, as a group, showed lower pain threshold scores and also lower pain tolerance scores. What Wise was also examining was an effect called Gender Role Expectations of Pain using a questionnaire to explore stereotypical expectations. As it turns out, the stronger the individual's identity with typical gender roles, the more likely the person was to follow expectations that fit with that gender. Women who identified strongly with stereotypical female traits had the lowest threshold and tolerance for pain, while women who did not identify with typical female traits scored more like the men in the study.

There are several possible explanations for differences in pain processing between men and women. Higher levels of estrogen and progesterone decrease pain tolerance. When women are at the point in the menstrual cycle where progesterone is highest (after ovulation), pain tolerance is typically lower. This is interesting since high-level young female gymnasts are typically much delayed in starting menstruation relative to other girls their age. Could it be that under the strain of intense demand (and often accompanying pain), delaying menstruation is a reasonable natural defense mechanism for pain tolerance?

Perhaps this is an evolutionary aspect of the typical roles of men and women. If one accepts the idea that males have typically assumed the role of hunters and warriors, a strong pain inhibition system would be a distinct advantage. For the female, greater sensitivity in general, especially the ability to empathize with another person, would make them much better at child rearing. This theory could be very far off the mark, but whatever the reason, the reality is that the ability to suppress pain is slightly less in women than in men. Shelley Taylor (Taylor *et al.* 2000) postulated that while the fight or flight paradigm is true primarily for males, females are more likely to adopt a "tend and befriend" model. Her research is fascinating and worth exploring.

On a lighter note, gender roles are clearly important in pain perception, as noted in a study by Levine and De Simone (1991). In this clever study, the researchers wondered whether a male would be less likely to report pain to an attractive young female investigator than they would to a male. Would you like to speculate how that study came out? Indeed, the males were willing to tolerate more pain in the presence of an attractive young female research assistant than they would otherwise. Who would have guessed?

In addition to gender, there are also cultural factors that clearly influence the experience of pain. There are clear variances in pain tolerances in both culture and ethnicity.

For instance, would it surprise you that the average decibel level in a Norwegian delivery room is less than the decibel level in a delivery room in Italy? (The famous line with respect to Norwegian pain tolerance is, "It hurt so much I almost said something...") Research also shows that African Americans and Latinos as a group have slightly lower pain tolerance levels than Caucasians (Wickelgren 2009).

One of my favorite examples of culture and pain tolerance has to do with childbirth and was written about by Dr. Patrick Wall (2000), one of the giants in the field of pain research. Have you ever heard the idea that childbirth, in its most natural state, is not pathology but something that should be non-traumatic? In this line of thinking, living close to nature and eating a natural diet would allow you to have an easy birthing process. This belief was developed (not always rightly so) out of the work of Grantly Dick-Read, in his book *Childbirth Without Fear* (2004). Witnessing the women of the north Kenyan area of Tulkarm leave their work, walk into the bushes, and birth a child with no sound at all, he surmised that natural childbirth could be relatively painless.

One ironic problem in this observation is that by most accounts, Dick-Read did not speak the Tulkarm language. Years later, a sociologist who spoke the language (okay, a female sociologist at that) revisited the same area and witnessed a similar birthing process, just as Dick-Read had done. When she asked the new mother if the birthing process (over there in the bushes) was painful, the woman reported that it was quite painful. When the scientist asked why the young woman did not cry out, her reply was, "It is not the custom of my people." What Dick-Read assumed to be the result of natural living may have had much more to do with culture than lack of pain. To be fair, his main point was that childbirth should not be something to be feared, because fear can increase pain. In this point, he was quite correct and did a wonderful service to women.

Culture, even at the family level, can have powerful influences on pain tolerance. If a parent or spouse is over-protective and over-sensitive, it can make the pain experience worse for their children. In one experiment, Dr. Jenny Tsao and colleagues (Chambers, Craig and Bennett 2002; Evans, Tsao and Zeltzer 2008) monitored the anxiety and pain tolerance levels of parents and children to laboratory pain testing. What Dr. Tsao found is that if the parents were anxious about the tests being performed on their children, the children were also anxious and thus experienced a lowered pain tolerance. Interestingly, this effect was true only for girls and not for boys! In this study, mothers were most often the parent who was represented, so that may seriously have influenced why boys were not affected. A study should probably be undertaken where fathers are present to see if their attitudes impact the pain experience of the son. Or perhaps mothers and daughters just have a finely tuned communication system…

On a final note, an excellent strategy in assessing the level of pain of patients was shared with me by Walter Laesch, a nurse anesthetist. Instead of asking patients how much pain they are experiencing on a scale of one to ten, he asks patients how comfortable they are on a scale of one to seven. This reframes the pain scale completely. As a result, less medication is needed. Brilliant, simple, and very effective.

CHAPTER 4

NOCERE AND THE ANATOMY OF PAIN

An early warning defense system

When comparing the old model of pain with the new understanding, it would seem logical that the major differences between the two reside largely in the psychological realm and pain perception, not the baseline physiology of pain. One would imagine that the basic physiology of pain is rather hardwired (and therefore accurate) and the perceptual/psychological aspects are where inappropriate responses to pain are possible. The reality, however, is that the mystery of pain begins in the most basic physiological functions of pain. We continue our journey there.

Many years ago, I had the great pleasure to tour the Nijo temple in Kyoto, Japan. The Nijo temple is a wooden structure, with wide hallways surrounding a central room. The central room is where the shogun resided, surrounded on all sides by this open-air hallway. There is no way into the center room except through the surrounding hallway. The wooden hallway is an amazing architectural feature called a Nightingale floor which was designed to squeak when walked upon. Even the weight of a cat causes the floor to squeak, thus alerting inhabitants in the interior to an unwanted intruder. The squeaking floor was an ancient security system, astounding both in its design and craftsmanship. The floor still squeaks today. Our modern-day security systems have essentially the same design principle:

put all the sensors in the periphery to warn in advance of any intruder.

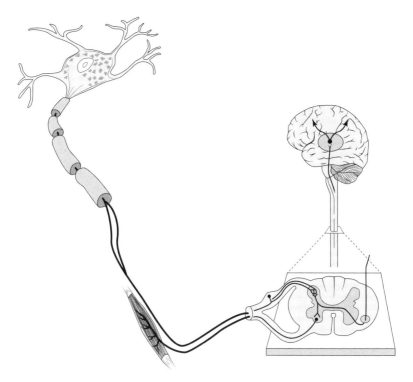

Figure 4.1: Nociceptors sense the presence of potential harmful stimuli in the skin, muscles, joints, and internal organs, most often sending that information up to the brain for processing and interpretation

Sensing potential threats in the body is very similar to the alarm system. You need sensors in the periphery to transmit information about potential threats as early as possible. Putting sensors next to your bed (or having the floor squeak in the center chamber) doesn't make much sense. It is a wee bit late at that point! Your body employs the same system: it puts the most sensors in your skin and superficial tissue to warn you before the potential threat invades the inner chambers and becomes a far more serious issue.

The sensors of potential damage in the body are called nociceptors, nerve cells that are specialized to react to a potentially noxious (injurious) stimulus. The origin of the word nociceptor comes from the Latin *nocere*, which means to harm. There are different kinds of nociceptors depending on where they are located in the body. The skin has essentially four types of nociceptors, each with an area of specialization.

1. *Mechanical.* These nociceptors respond to pinching, cutting, stretching, etc.

2. *Thermal.* These nociceptors respond to potentially dangerous temperature changes.

3. *Chemical.* These nociceptors respond to irritating substances like capsaicin from red peppers.

4. *Polymodal.* This category can respond to any of the previous three types (mechanical, thermal, chemical). It is like a free agent which can do any of the jobs available.

While the skin has many nociceptors, other areas also need protection against possible threats, as described below.

Joint nociceptors

As you might imagine, a joint in the body needs to know if there is a potential threat to its health and existence. These threats are most likely to come as a result of increased pressure inside the joint, such as compression or twisting under pressure. Therefore, these nociceptors are primarily mechanosensitive. Since a joint like the knee is under a fair amount of pressure when we jump or run, the threshold for these pressure receptors is often very high.

One more type of nociceptor in a joint, called a 'silent' nociceptor, is activated in the presence of inflammation. These receptors lie in wait and are activated by chemicals released during the inflammatory process. When silent nociceptors come online, they and the mechanosensitive nociceptors have a dramatically reduced threshold to movement and pressure. For example, imagine straining your knee during a fall. Before the trauma, you could painlessly jump up and down with no reaction to the increased pressure in the joint. After the trauma, the reactive threshold of the mechanoreceptors and newly recruited silent receptors is lowered so much that taking a step with the injured leg is painful. These nociceptors are now responding to extremely small stimuli, a much exaggerated response.

Visceral (internal organ) nociceptors

Remember how the greatest need for alarm sensors is in the periphery of your property? While the skin has a very dense assortment of the four types of nociceptors, internal organs have the same four types in dramatically fewer numbers. As a result of having more nociceptors, the skin has much greater capability to experience pain than do internal organs. Not having a strong voice (nociception) themselves, internal organs often use the periphery as the sounding board for pain. When the internal organ experiences pain or inflammation, it uses an area with greater nociception to sound the alarm. These pains can be quite a mystery, unless one is trained to recognize the language of internal organ pain.

Each internal organ refers to a specific part of the peripheral body, typically a muscle or anatomical region. These referral patterns are well known to physicians who use that information to trace which internal organ has a problem. For example, the gall bladder, having few nociceptors itself, often refers pain to the right shoulder-blade. Stomach cancer, which may develop completely silently, may present as a pain between the shoulders long before it is diagnosed. A kidney problem may present as back pain and a problem with the spleen may present as a stitch in the side. The pain from a heart problem is well known: pain down the left arm and chest, or sudden pain in the jaw. The areas that have an abundance of sensors become the sounding board for the parts of our body which have very few. It is a physician's job to interpret the presenting symptoms and uncover the real source of pain.

Pain that is referred can be mysterious and enormously frustrating. How does one know when a pain between the shoulders is a stomach problem and when is it simply muscular tightness? There are two simple criteria that physicians often use: mechanical pain and associated phenomena.

Mechanical pain is pain that is made better or worse with movement or position. If the source of your mid-back pain is a muscle, then stretching, contracting, or positioning that muscle differently should change the pain. Your stomach, though, doesn't really care how you move, it just hurts. If no position or action makes the pain better or worse, there is serious cause for concern.

An associated phenomenon refers to a symptom that accompanies the original pain but comes from a different body system. If you have constant pain between the shoulders, have you also noticed any digestive concerns? Has there been unintended weight loss? When a physician asks patients questions, he/she is looking for additional clues that might shed more light on possible internal organ difficulties. Make sure to give your doctor all the information you can. What may seem unrelated to you may be a big clue for your physician.

Just like joints, there are also "silent" nociceptors in the viscera, ready to be activated if there is any inflammation present. When there is some problem, such as an infection, silent nociceptors activate and the whole system becomes hyper-reactive. A bladder infection is an excellent example of this phenomenon. Normally, as urine accumulates in the bladder, the stretching of the walls of the bladder signal the need to evacuate. During an infection, the silent nociceptors activate quickly and, as a result, even a small amount of fluid triggers the need to urinate.

Pain receptors?

You may notice that I do not refer to nociceptors simply as pain receptors, something that would be easy but perhaps, in a way, slightly incorrect to do. This may seem like a semantic ploy, but one that makes an important point. Take, for instance, the aforementioned rare defect called Congenital Indifference to Pain (CIP). There is some evidence that in many of these people, the nociceptors are present and working normally, but the brain does not interpret the sensation as painful. Instead, someone with CIP may feel the pain of a broken bone as simply a feeling of pressure. While it is the job of nociceptors to sense, it is the job of the brain to interpret the *meaning* of what is sensed. Proper functioning of the system can go awry at both the peripheral level (sensing) and at the level of interpretation (the brain). Thus begins the mystery of pain even at the most basic level, that of picking up the signal (called transduction).

Referring back to the home alarm system analogy, the sensors at the edges of your property are likely to be motion detectors. Sensing a bit of motion, they send a signal back to a control center to trigger an alarm. If the motion is from your vertical blinds, which are waving because of air movement from a vent or fan, triggering the police to come is not productive. The technician who installed your system tunes it to recognize only larger movement so that the motion of your drapes from the ceiling fan should not set off the alarm. The difference between intruder and drapery motion is an important distinction, one that the outward sensors cannot make without something telling them how sensitive to be.

In the body, nociceptors also respond to stimuli that they perceive as *potentially* damaging. While detecting actual damage is relatively straightforward, potential damage leaves *a lot* of room for error. If you are walking in a familiar town, you may not see strangers as potential threats, even though you know nothing about these people. On the other hand, walking down a street in a seedy neighborhood may make you see everyone as a threat, which may or may not be true. A potential threat means the line can be drawn anywhere, for varying reasons at varying times. This dilemma is what makes an insurgency conflict so much different from a traditional war where the identity of the enemy is very clear. Perhaps most importantly, the tendency to mistake a non-combatant for a true threat is obviously very high.

Nociceptors, like those motion sensors, cannot make subtle distinctions about the stimuli that they respond to. They simply pick up messages; they don't read or interpret them. The interpretation of the data happens in the brain, not the periphery. For the nociceptors, the volume and the number of nociceptors firing are equated to the severity of the threat. In our motion sensors, small motions of the vertical blinds might be from the ceiling fan, larger motions from an intruder. If nociceptors are firing vigorously or large numbers of them are active, the brain perceives that a major threat is in progress.

There are specialized types of nerves that pick up sensory information in the periphery and send them to the brain for processing. Nerves called *A alpha*, *A beta*, and *A delta* are involved in the perception of touch, temperature, chemical sensations, and information as to where you are in space, which is called proprioception. Additionally, neuro-receptors called C fibers account for most nociception. Since our interest is in pain, we will focus on the two types of nerves that play a role in pain, the A delta and C fibers. The large A delta receptors transmit information about intense pressure or temperature and do so at lightning speed. If you step off a curb incorrectly, you get a jolt of pain from the A delta fibers telling you that your ankle is about to be injured. The speed of the signal through the A delta fibers helps you to react immediately to minimize any damage. Shortly thereafter, there follows a slow, deep, and perhaps burning pain, letting you know that you really did sprain your ankle. This secondary sensation is C fiber pain. Most nociception (about 70%) is done by C fibers; their prevalence and special qualities make them central to our experience of chronic pain.

Source location

When you experience a deep aching pain where the source is difficult to locate, the chances are high that the pain was travelling through the C fiber network. Until I really understood the significance of this, I missed an important point in caring for clients who have pain. Often, when I have asked clients the exact location of their pain, the answers are often so vague as to border on being useless. At this point, I have often thought that the person must have a poor sense of his/her body, which makes me wonder if that is a part of the reason he/she is in pain.

I have come to the realization that this idea is fundamentally wrong (though an element of it may be true for a different reason) because of the nature of C fiber pain. Identifying where you were hit by a baseball is not difficult: your accuracy will be perfect and point-specific. The discomfort of the initial hit uses the A delta network, which is very point-specific. Chronic pain uses the C fiber network which, by its very nature, has poor location specificity. The person who I thought had a poor sense of his/her body was instead telling me what kind of pain he/she had.

Time

If, for example, you are walking on a beach and feel a sharp sensation on your foot, the neural signal sent from the foot travels at lightning speed. In contrast, the C fiber transmission system is slow, *really slow*, traveling at a lesser speed than most people walk. Any interaction with the C fiber network is going to take more processing time, in stark contrast to interaction with the other neural networks.

You may have had this experience during a manual physical examination by a therapist or physician looking for tender areas. If the therapist or doctor moves quickly from spot to spot on your body, you may have difficulty comparing the sensitivity from place to place. You may find yourself saying something like, "Well, three spots back was actually pretty tender." By the time your brain was able to process that information, the examiner had moved on to a new area. The C fiber system is slow; therefore interacting with it should also be done very slowly.

Next, let's examine how nociceptors behave when they respond inappropriately, which is what chronic pain is all about.

CHAPTER 5

WHEN THE SYSTEM GOES AWRY

Peripheral and central sensitization

The human nervous system is finely tuned to protect the organism from harm. Like any sensitive and complex system, little problems have *massive* consequences. The system can be distorted at both the periphery, where information is gathered, and at the central nervous system (CNS), where information is processed. Worse yet, each one can reinforce the other, creating a disastrous cascade of events.

Peripheral sensitization: Deputizing more nociceptors…

In the last chapter, we looked at several kinds of sensory nerves in peripheral tissue, specifically focusing on the process of nociception. We used the example of a motion detector to represent sensory nerves. Setting the level at which these nerves fire is referred to as neural sensitivity. When the level of sensitivity becomes too high, the receptors at the periphery become hypersensitive to *any* kind of stimulus. This state of inappropriate firing is called peripheral sensitization, a condition in which normal stimuli can be misinterpreted as noxious when in reality they are not.

If you remember, C fiber sensory nerves account for about 70 percent of nociception. The rest of nociception comes from

A delta nerves, which are normally touch receptors. When there is heightened sensitivity, these receptors perceive touch as painful, rather than just pressure alone. Clinicians and researchers call this condition *allodynia*.

You probably have personal experience with this effect, perhaps after an injury or when you have been under lots of stress. In a gesture of kindness, your spouse gives your shoulders a squeeze and your response is to recoil in pain. At that point your spouse gives you that "Hey, I was just trying to help!" look. In fact, at another time, the same pressure would feel comforting, but not when the system is sensitized. Welcome to the world of allodynia.

Part of the genius of the design of the body is that very few receptors are specialized to just one task. This is protective and gives the system multiple options in case one part fails. Having A delta receptors capable of nociception is protective, but only if additional nociception is absolutely needed. If it is employed consistently, the A delta fibers are going to misinterpret information because they "expect" to.

For example, imagine if a town sheriff had the ability to deputize citizens to help control drivers that speed in a community. Given this new mission, what are the odds that these new deputies would be hyper-vigilant for speeders? Do you think the rate of speeding tickets might go up in exact proportion to the number of new deputies? Where a seasoned police officer may allow a cushion for drivers that are moving with the traffic flow, the new deputies may not be so forgiving. Hey, speeding is speeding.

So it is with the newfound nociceptors. A stimulus that normally isn't painful is now really uncomfortable. If you're that person for whom light touch is now perceived as painful, for instance, it makes no sense. If this is a temporary condition as a result of a trauma, the sensitivity will abate in exact proportion to healing. Unfortunately, in chronic conditions like fibromyalgia, the sensitivity stays heightened. Worse yet, when the central nervous system sees how much nociception (speeding tickets) keeps flooding in, it doesn't tone down the system; it will increase resources (more deputies) to deal with the escalating problem it perceives. The system cycles out of control quickly.

Heightened sensitivity

In the nervous system, the point at which a nerve senses stimuli is not constant. Just as we can train our senses to listen more closely to a piece of music, picking out the secondary accompaniment hidden behind the melody, our nociceptive capability can also be heightened or dampened. As we saw in the last paragraph, if you look for speeders you will probably find them.

One of the ways that sensitivity can be a problem is that, over time, nociceptors can essentially "learn" to respond faster to the same stimuli. If you have had a bit of sunburn, your skin is sensitized to heat. The moderately hot water of a shower can be absolutely excruciating, even though that temperature is something that normally feels quite pleasant. The more you experience a specific stimulus as painful, the more likely it is that your nociceptors will be sensitized to that experience. If a particular exercise or movement causes you pain each time you do it, you will be quite reluctant to do anything that resembles that movement in the future.

In chronic pain, the template can be applied far too broadly. Anything remotely similar to the original offending movement will also be perceived as problematic. Revisiting the earlier analogy about a foot soldier in dangerous territory, a reasonable survival strategy in such a dangerous context is to regard everyone as a possible combatant. This will result in three possible outcomes that often coexist: the soldier will survive longer in the immediate danger area, non-combatants will probably be killed, and the long-term cost of hyper-vigilance can have deleterious effects on the soldier. These same effects also happen in the experience of pain. The broad application of questionable stimuli can be very protective in acute pain. Unfortunately, innocent stimuli are misperceived as the enemy and the system wears down over time.

Probably the best example of peripheral sensitivity is something I did for a lecture several years ago. In looking for an example to illustrate peripheral sensitivity, I had a sudden inspiration. I told my group a complete fabrication to illustrate how peripheral sensitization happens. I apologized to the group for not conveying an announcement the hotel had asked me to share earlier that morning. The hotel had suggested not putting anything with food or any personal belongings (such as purses or briefcases) on the floor as the facility had been having a problem with roach infestation (I am not sure the hotel would have appreciated this). The scramble was on; people grabbed their belongings and set them on an open table or chair. As I was speaking for the next 15 minutes, I could see the eyes of the participants scanning the floor for movement. At this point, I asked if anyone else besides me had actually seen a cockroach. About half the class raised a hand. When I explained the ruse, they looked less than thrilled, but I think they will never forget the point. If sensitivity gets turned up too high, innocuous stimuli (small movements out of the corner of the eye) can easily be misinterpreted as a problem (roaches are everywhere).

Winding up the system through repetition

In our security system analogy used earlier, we generally assume that there is one intruder trying to access the property and a resultant warning sign, like a siren, will scare the intruder away. In the body, however, the stimulus doesn't let up after just one event. What happens to the sensory system if the intruder just keeps coming? What if there is more than one intruder and they come in waves? This possibility sets up a cascade of events in the sensing system, one which is often out of proportion to the initial stimulus. In a famous experiment, pain researcher (and one of the true giants of the field) Patrick Wall (Wall and Woolf 1984) showed that if you excited a C fiber neuron once, it was sensitized for up to three minutes. If it was stimulated once a second for 20 seconds, it was hypersensitive for up to *90* minutes. In our analogy of a foot soldier on patrol, if the soldier sees a potential threat once a second for 20 seconds, that soldier will see everything as a threat for the next hour and a half.

The increasing neural sensitivity from repetition is called *wind-up* and it affects us more than you think. Here is a simple experiment to try. Take a pen (with the point retracted) or something mildly pointed and press into your forearm, hard enough to leave an impression in the tissue. Once every second, press right back in the same place (as noted by the impression) with exactly the same amount of force. (Do this about 10–12 times.) Notice how the sensitivity increases? This is wind-up in action. Although the stimulus is the same, the sensitivity increases. Granted, there probably is a point in time where you acclimate to the discomfort, but don't try that!

Wind-up is one of the aspects of C fibers that make them so unusual. In essence, it isn't just the intensity of the event; it is also the *frequency* of the noxious stimuli that can escalate the pain experience. Finding some way to interrupt the frequency of the offending stimulus may be of vital importance in stopping the cascade of pain caused by wind-up. Whether that strategy is a break in activity, taking some medication to dampen the pain, or quiet meditation, interrupting the onslaught of stimuli could be very helpful.

Chemicals and sensitivity

Once a nociceptor has been activated, various chemicals are released into the surrounding tissue. These chemicals, some of which are histamine, serotonin, prostaglandins, globulin and protein kinases, and potassium ions further sensitize the surrounding area. Often, these substances don't just activate the nociceptors of the injured site, they lower the threshold of sensitivity in *surrounding* nociceptors. This lowered sensitivity makes the neighboring nociceptors fire at low intensity stimuli, or stimuli that aren't even noxious. In our alarm system analogy, the peripheral sensors could release a substance that makes nearby sensors fire too quickly at objects that aren't even intruders. In which case, a simple touch to the injured area or change in temperature can feel very painful. (Imagine putting a shirt on over sunburned shoulders—normally the cloth brushing over your skin is not painful.)

Once a potentially dangerous stimulus has been perceived at the periphery, the information is sent to a special area of the spinal cord called the dorsal horn. This upward flow of information from the periphery to the brain is called *afferent* information. This afferent data is sent via the spinal cord to various parts of the brain that deal with pain processing, which then decide how to respond to this information coming from the periphery. Here again, the normally protective mechanisms of acute pain can escalate out of control in the chronic pain state.

Modulation: Why does scratching an itch feel so good?

Perhaps it is reflective of my age, but every time I think of pain processing I think of the comedian Lily Tomlin. Ms. Tomlin portrayed this wonderful character in her comedy routines, a switchboard operator for a phone system. (For my younger friends, a switchboard operator is one who routed incoming phone calls. He/she would sit in front of a large board and as calls came in, lights would flash indicating activity on that phone line. The switchboard operator would direct the calls to the correct extension.) What made this particular routine so funny is that switchboard operators were supposed to be rather robotic—one did not think of them as having anything to add to the task of simply routing a call to the right person. In her role, she offered opinions and sarcastic comments, and exercised some interesting judgment calls while answering the phone. She exercised power and control, even when her job was simply to route a call to the correct person.

Our brains have areas that are very much like that: instead of just routing information, they often add something to the data. Far from being simply a router, they influence the neural input routed through them. Like a call routed through Ms. Tomlin, the output can be different from what was originally intended or expected. Changing neural information along the way, making the signal stronger or weaker, is called modulation. In neural terms, *excitation* refers to turning up the volume and *inhibition* refers to turning down the volume of sensory data.

Nerves that are hyper-excitable are the source of much of the pain that we experience. A reasonable treatment strategy to combat over-excitation is neural inhibition (turning down the volume), but that is where treating pain suddenly gets very messy and difficult. Decreasing the volume level (inhibition) is very difficult to accomplish selectively. The ideal strategy is to target the over-excited neural area and dampen *only* those nerves. Unfortunately, this turns out to be extremely challenging.

When you turn the volume down en masse, scientists call this *post-synaptic inhibition*. Post-synaptic inhibition is a great way to lower the neural firing, except for one small problem: *every* stimulus is dampened. Anyone who has ingested powerful pain medicine knows first-hand about post-synaptic inhibition. While the neural firing of pain is lowered, so is the ability to drive a car or function normally in life. Every neural stimulus gets inhibited at the same rate, not selectively the ones involved in the experience of pain. This is the bane of most pharmacological approaches to pain relief. What everyone wants is a drug that is highly selective for the pain and leaves everything else untouched. This is the Holy Grail of pharmacology research and pain. Unfortunately, this isn't quite possible yet.

Another form of pain reduction works by turning *up* the volume somewhere else. This form of inhibition is called *pre-synaptic inhibition*. This strategy can be enormously helpful in dealing with pain and warrants a closer look.

Every parent has probably employed a pre-synaptic inhibition strategy at some point in child-rearing, as in the following example. While at the grocery checkout lane, your child decides to have a tantrum and people in surrounding checkout lanes are now staring at your child. "Look, a giraffe in the parking lot!" you exclaim. "Oh, you just missed him." (True, we could have called this strategy distraction, but pre-synaptic inhibition sounds so much more impressive!)

This always makes me think of a flight I was on a few years ago. A mother was having a very difficult time with her young son, who was screaming and crying. The attendant came over and calmly sat with the boy, giving the mother a moment of relief. The attendant showed this child to the window, and began to point out roads, buildings, and cars on the ground below. Pretty soon, he was spotting these objects with regularity and his mood had totally changed. I will always remember him pointing out a school bus and having half the plane (mostly men traveling on business) leaning out the window to see if they too could spot it.

These examples of pre-synaptic inhibition deal with attention, but can the same process be used with physical pain? The answer is absolutely yes, and again, you have probably already used this approach. Imagine a little league baseball player getting hit on the leg with an errant pitch. What is the first thing that a coach will do? The coach will vigorously rub the leg which was hit by the baseball. Why would rubbing the leg decrease the pain? Remember the discussion about the different sensory nerves and their varying speeds of transmission? The sensory fibers that transmit the data from vigorous rubbing are far faster than the deep aching pain from getting hit with a pitch. The louder/faster signals win in the attention game.

This same phenomenon is probably at the core of itching, a fascinating neural process in and of itself. When bitten by a mosquito, it is nearly impossible to restrain oneself from scratching the area of the bite. Why does scratching feel so good? Without the itch, scratching so vigorously wouldn't feel satisfying, it would be painful. The word "scratch" should be our clue that pre-synaptic inhibition is taking place. We don't just touch the area, we scratch. The greater the itch, the more vigorously we scratch. Scratching floods the sensory system with data that overwhelms the itch experience (hopefully).

This idea of a stronger input overwhelming a lesser input is at the heart of the *gate control* theory of pain, proposed by scientists Patrick Wall and Ronald Melzack (1965). Strong input from large receptive fields tends to inhibit the smaller, more defined input coming from a specific source of pain. From rubbing an elbow when one of our children falls down to the use of Transcutaneous Electrical Nerve Stimulation (TENS) units to control chronic pain, the gate control theory was an enormous contribution to the understanding of pain.

Up to this point, we have examined how information is picked up in the periphery and potentially changed en route. Once the brain receives the afferent input from the periphery, it responds by sending information back down the neural system. This downward flow of information is called *efferent* processing. This is the brain's way of telling the body how to respond to that which is perceived. In a normal process, the brain instructs the body to pull away from danger, charge ahead, or freeze until the danger is over. The fight, flight, freeze model is a simplified but fairly accurate model of nervous system reaction. The most important point is that the brain must tell the body *how to respond* to the situation given the information present.

Central sensitization: Mom's having a really bad day...

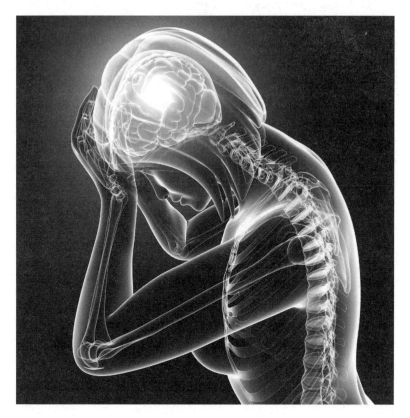

Figure 5.1: Sensitization can happen at the central nervous system as well as in the periphery. When the central nervous system is hyper-excitable, it responds in an exaggerated way to innocuos inputs. This hyper-responsiveness increases the sensitivity of the periphery as well, creating a vicious cycle.

In the previous section, we explored how the threshold at which nerves respond to a stimulus can change; the effect of lowering the threshold is called peripheral sensitivity. The same process of increased sensitivity can also take place in the central processing regions of the brain as well. Central sensitization is defined as an amplification of neural signaling within the central nervous system (CNS) that elicits pain hypersensitivity. Like peripheral sensitization, central sensitization is a protective process gone awry. If the number or intensity of the perceived threats is high, it only makes sense for the system to go on high-alert status.

Also explored in the previous section was post-synaptic inhibition, turning down (inhibiting) the sensitivity levels of the nervous system en masse. The problem with post-synaptic inhibition is that it turns down the volume on *everything*, not just in the area that hurts. Central sensitization is the exact opposite situation: it turns *up* the sensitivity level en masse, not just at the area of injury. Understanding this process is vital to the treatment of pain syndromes such as migraines and fibromyalgia, which are both thought to have their origins in the process of central sensitization.

There are three effects of central sensitization, according to Dr. Clifford Woolf (2011): it lowers the firing threshold, the after-effects of pain tend to linger, and input from surrounding uninjured tissue may also be interpreted as noxious. Let's begin by exploring the first component, how central sensitization lowers the threshold of the system as a whole, not just the injured area.

Mom's having a bad day...

In general, parents strive to be fair in disciplining their children. If you talk to children with multiple siblings, however, you may hear a very different story. Kids know that when Mom is in a bad mood, everyone is bound to suffer. In defense of the mother, it is very hard to direct frustration solely to the misbehaving child. The more frustrated and angry the mother becomes, the more likely it is that she will be overly sensitive to the fairly normal behavior of the non-involved children as well. When Mom loses her cool, everybody suffers. So it is with central sensitization.

A wonderful example of central sensitization and its effect on multiple areas of the body was revealed by Freeman (Freeman, Nystrom, and Centeno 2009). The researchers explored how injuries to the neck may affect tissues in other parts of the body as well. Dr. Freeman and his colleagues examined people who had neck muscle injuries and measured not only the degree to which these neck muscle injuries affected neck movement, but also the sensitivity to pressure (touch) in other parts of the body (a shoulder muscle, an arm muscle, and a leg muscle). Once the painful areas of tissue in the neck were neutralized via injection techniques, the distant areas of the body were also then less sensitive to pressure. The most reasonable explanation is that input from the neck excited regions of the brain, which then spread sensitivity to the peripheral areas (shoulder, arm, leg) measured in the study.

Mom's still a bit on edge...

Once there has been some sort of blow-up, the aftermath doesn't disappear immediately. In our irritated mom analogy, everyone is still walking on eggshells after the blow-up. Children are careful what they say and do for fear that it will be interpreted as insolent behavior. In central sensitization, the same lingering of the pain experience occurs. In animal studies, for instance, once a painful experience has been repeated often enough, the brain "learns" to respond more quickly to anything that *might* be interpreted as pain. Since the brain has learned to react more quickly to that which may be painful, the likelihood it will react inappropriately to a completely harmless stimulus is very high. Due to the frequency of perceived danger (little of it actually real), the brain perceives a constant onslaught of possible threats, which then validates continuing the hyper-excited state.

For this reason, central sensitization is often self-sustaining. An essential point here is that the offending stimulus *need no longer be present* to sustain the effect; anything that resembles it will keep the system hyper-vigilant. The more entrenched central sensitization becomes, the more self-sustaining it is. Like a child afraid of the night, every sound and shadow confirms the presence of monsters out there somewhere. Exasperated and fatigued parents may try to reason with the child, but fear governs perception.

Like calming a frightened child to sleep, getting the nervous system out of central sensitization can be incredibly difficult. Most importantly, if at all possible, every reasonable strategy should be employed to prevent central sensitization from happening in the first place. How can that be accomplished? Often, the simplest answer is pre-emptive pain control before the pain becomes too entrenched.

As an example, I once treated a woman who had a fairly severe back injury and for several reasons did not follow her doctor's advice. She decided to tough out the pain, not wanting to take anything to reduce it. While not taking medication for pain may seem noble at first glance, the end result was disastrous. Her nervous system became extremely sensitized. When I touched anywhere on her back, she would flinch with anticipation of pain. Asking her if the places I was touching were actually painful, she admitted they were not. Her exaggerated response was applied across the board: to my touch, to temperature, to movement. Every input, even my touch, was a potential threat. Treatment went incredibly slowly and incrementally. As you might imagine, treating central sensitization after the fact is much more difficult than preventing it in the first place. In fact, a study by Dr. Clifford Woolf (Richmond, Bromley, and Woolf 1993) showed that once central sensitization exists, it takes *ten times* the medication to abolish it than if pain medicine had been given initially to prevent it.

As an example of preventing central sensitization, one research study by Dr. Woolf (Richmond *et al.* 1993) gave small doses of morphine to women along with normal anesthesia before a hysterectomy. Those women who received this small dose of pre-emptive morphine used much less pain control medication after surgery and had less pain around the surgical wound. While this study involved using a drug (morphine), it is reasonable to assume than any pain control strategy that decreases central nervous system activity before surgery would help to create favorable outcomes post-surgery.

The way the brain responds to a stimulus is in large part based on the brain's perceived meaning of that stimulus. As you might imagine, here is where the "pain train" can really jump the tracks. Accurate perceptions produce perfectly appropriate responses; errant perceptions can lead us far astray.

Chapter 6

THE IMPORTANCE OF MEANING AND CONTEXT
The stories we tell ourselves

"Man is a credulous animal, and must believe something; in the absence of good grounds for belief, he will be satisfied with bad ones."

Bertrand Russell

Let us begin by imagining some scenarios:

Imagine, as you are reading this, that you begin to feel a stinging sensation on your thigh. As the stinging commands your attention, you glance down at your leg to see a mosquito happily feasting on your flesh. Brushing the mosquito away, you vow not to leave the front door open again for any length of time.

Imagine this same scenario, this time with one difference. As you feel the stinging on your thigh, there is no mosquito present when you look at your leg. In fact, there doesn't seem to be any visible reason for the pain you are feeling. You move, thinking that maybe shifting positions will help, but it does not. Your brain can come up with no reasonable cause for what you are experiencing.

Next, compare these two scenarios which exemplify the importance of context:

You are sitting at home working away on a project you could not finish at work. Being totally fatigued, but pressing on, you keep working away at the report on your screen. Suddenly, you are aware of a gentle touch brushing the back of your hair and soothing your shoulders, trying to comfort you and remind you how late the hour has become. The touch of your spouse's hand is a comforting reminder to come to bed.

You are sitting on the subway in New York City, the first time you have taken the subway by yourself. Confident you are on the correct train, you settle in to read the morning paper. Suddenly, you feel a hand brushing lightly over the back of your head and the top of your shoulders. You freeze…

Think about how your brain would respond to these different scenarios. In the first of the two involving thigh pain, you have the sensation of pain, a reason or cause, an action, and a resolution. In the second, you have a sensation, no obvious reason, and subsequently no appropriate response. The reason the first scenario (where the cause for pain is obvious) is preferable to you is the result of the innate wiring in the brain.

In the second group of scenarios involving context, the experience of a gentle touch on your shoulder is very different depending on the context in which it is experienced. Simply put, context defines meaning.

Every time I think of meaning and pain, I cannot help but consider the biblical story of Job. Job, a righteous and law-abiding man, is besieged by suffering and the betrayal of both his body and seemingly of the God that created it. His struggle is our struggle; his immediate desire is to understand *why* he is suffering. (For a wonderful treatise on this subject, read the 2003 book *Job's Body* by Deane Juhan.)

Job is a man who has the world figured out, a man who is wise and universally admired by his peers and his family.

His belief is that the world is a predictable place, where cause and effect are clearly linked. His success, as seen through his eyes, is a manifestation of understanding those rules and putting them into practice. Unfortunately, as investment houses tend to say, "Past performance is not predictive of future gains." This was especially true for Job. His world was about to be turned upside-down.

For seemingly no reason, Job's world begins to fall apart. His health begins to fail, his family, his estate, everything he values is crumbling and nothing in his arsenal of understanding can make any sense of it. Job is left with two possible explanations. The first explanation (and the one put forth by his "friends") is that he must have done something to incur this terrible plight. (Back to the "pain as punishment" model.) The other possibility is that the problem lies outside himself in a faulty world or a Creator that has made a terrible mistake. In other words, God goofed and is not to be trusted.

Somewhere in the struggle, Job comes to a different conclusion, one in which he confronts his previous model of the world with a new understanding. Job comes to see that his struggle and the introspection that followed have deepened his spiritual understanding. His questioning and arguing with God suddenly gave him insight into a dynamic world that was lived, not just perceived.

Beyond Job's insights, I would like to focus on his deep desire to explain his suffering. What Job's rational mind desired was a clear connection between whatever he did and the suffering he is experiencing. This desire for meaning is a primal need of our brain; we want clear relationships between action and consequence. This need for clear causal relationships is the double-edged sword that makes us both wise and often very foolish. The human brain does not deal well with randomness, we need reasons for everything. If no reasonable explanation is available, we make one up.

The importance of meaning reinforces the concept that pain is not merely a stimulus, just as the touch of another person is not merely a stimulus. The context and perceived meaning of what is experienced is just as important as the stimulus itself, perhaps more so. As we have explored, at the most basic level the neural inputs that could be noxious are received by the nociceptors. The nociceptors then send these inputs up to the brain for clarification of meaning. The peripheral receptors do not make judgments about the nature of the stimulus, just that it exists. It is the brain that decides what the meaning of the stimulus is and how to respond. Essentially, it isn't pain until the brain says it's pain.

This concept of pain as perception is at the heart of this book for a very important reason. If pain is a stimulus (a clear painful input which then causes a negative reaction), there is little that can be done to alter this experience. The two available choices would be to stop the offending stimulus (easy to say, hard to do) or to dull the receptors of the stimulus (which tends to dull many more functions than just pain perception). On the other hand, if pain is a perception, there are numerous ways that the experience can be altered, both for better and for worse. This empowers us.

Perceptions can be changed in a multitude of ways, whereas the stimulus model leaves us few choices. There is, however, a danger in applying the "pain as perception" model too broadly. Linking pain to perception is often misinterpreted by the public as a way of inferring that the pain they are experiencing is somehow in their mind, and therefore less real. This can be interpreted by the pain sufferer as invalidation—and pain sufferers do not need another way to be invalidated. They have had enough already.

If I may, I wish to parallel the perception/stimulus model of pain with an old model of thinking about emotions and health. As the field of psychoimmunology began to develop, there was an understanding that how we think affects our physiology. If our thoughts are intensely negative, then what follows are a whole set of undesirable (and measurable) physiological consequences. Unfortunately, some people in the field started to come from the other direction, meaning that if you were sick then the illness is the ultimate result of negative emotions or certain thinking patterns. Instead of empowering people by teaching psychological strategies to maximize health, these people made the sick person feel guilty for being sick. Thankfully, we have moved beyond that dark chapter of limited understanding. (Obviously, we have not completely moved beyond it. I recently returned from speaking at a conference where the keynote speaker asserted that the way you think can give you cancer. Sadly, remnants of this thinking die hard.)

With respect to pain, there is a similar danger. If pain is largely about perception, then how real is it? Sit on a tack and let's have that discussion! Perception *is* reality. If someone says something to me that I find devastating, it does not matter if he did not intend it to be insulting; the effect of the statement was uncomfortable. In communication, there is a saying, "The meaning of a communication is the response received." In pain, perception creates very real experiences; that experience is just as real even if the offending cause is not obvious. One of the most, if not *the* most, important guidelines for the practitioner who treats people in pain is this: "Patients are always in as much pain as they say they are." It is tempting for healthcare providers or the family of a person in pain to say that a seemingly harmless activity or stimulus should not, or could not, result in such pain. Reactions, however, are seldom in a linear relationship to the stimulus intensity that caused them, but reactions are reality.

With regard to the perception of pain, if you complain of leg pain and I see a tack sticking out of your thigh, I am pretty sure I know the cause of your malady. If I am the healthcare provider, I remove the tack, allow the tissue to heal, and commend myself for such an insightful observation. The meaning of your pain is aligned to what I can observe with my eyes or feel through physical examination.

In our healthcare system, we want everything to have biomedical roots. If there is no observable pathology, suddenly doubt enters into the process. Imagine being a physician and having a patient who describes a myriad of painful symptoms, yet the provider can find no obvious reason for the patient's suffering. If the physician is not careful, the easiest path to take is to doubt the validity of the pain. In a sense, the thinking is, "If I can't see it, you don't have it."

This may sound a little over the top, but for many of you reading this book it is an all too familiar experience. Some of you may have flashed back to some pretty painful encounters with healthcare providers who gently (or not so gently) asserted that your pain was really somewhere in the six inches between your ears. (I can't help but think of a gravesite, where the epitaph reads, "I told you I was ill.") This denial of the patient's experience of pain is the height of clinical arrogance, yet it happens too frequently.

Many people with unexplained pain have experienced doubt not only from their doctor but from family and friends too. Think of the internal conflict these pain sufferers have (perhaps you know this all too well); if everyone doubts you, you now start to doubt yourself. Then, the pain hits, and the other part of you knows this suffering is very real; it is certainly not imaginary. Not only do you feel bad, you feel bad about feeling bad. All this suffering occurs simply because meaning cannot be ascribed to your symptoms since a cause cannot be seen.

Errant meanings

There was a book published a few years ago with a great title, *How We Know What Isn't So* (Gilovitch 1993). I think of that phrase often, especially as it applies to pain. Unfortunately, the need to have clear causality often plays a role in serious misunderstandings about pain. People commonly ascribe reasons for their pain that are far from reality, but at least they have the comfort of believing in a cause for their suffering. Below are some common ones.

Pain and aging

Blindly attributing muscular aches and pain to aging is a common experience in my office. Hundreds of times, I have sat across from clients who unequivocally state that the reason for their pain is the fact that they are old. (You'd be surprised at the wide range of what people think is old!) While at some level this is fairly reasonable, most of the time it is not applicable to the cause of their particular pain. When a client complains of pain in his right shoulder due to aging, I can't resist asking about the health of the left shoulder. Typically, the response is that the left shoulder never gives them trouble. I love the look on the client's face when I ask him how old the left shoulder is.

It must be the last thing I did

When people are in pain and that pain is a result of a movement, the temptation is to ascribe the cause of the pain to the very last activity done. When a guy who is six feet three inches tall and built like a tank tells me that his back went into a spasm while he was putting on his socks, his brain is inclined to think the spasm is due to the action of putting on socks. I am often tempted to suggest he buy lighter socks. It often doesn't occur to people to consider the last offending activity to be the proverbial straw that broke the camel's back.

What created the pain in many situations is often a series of events, all of which predisposed a certain body structure to be sensitized to the simplest of actions. Consider the following presentation of back pain I saw recently.

Ms. B presented with back pain as a result of lifting her grandchild. Babysitting at her daughter's house, she was lifting her grandchild over a doggie gate when her back suddenly went into a spasm. Lifting the child over the gate was mechanically quite awkward, but she had done this numerous times before without incident.

The backdrop to this particular bout of pain was important. A few weeks earlier, she tripped and severely strained her knee. The knee had improved greatly, but was not yet fully healed. It is also important that she had had previous bouts of back spasms, one every few years or so.

Lifting her grandchild over the doggie gate was a serious load on the low back musculature, but she had done this before without pain. This time, however, her ailing knee (and thus her leg) did not give her a full base of support. This lack of support required her already overburdened back muscles to do even more, which resulted in a severe spasm.

If we drew an equation to represent Ms. B's back pain, it might look like this:

$$\text{Prior history of back pain (PH)} + \text{Knee injury (KI)} +$$
$$\text{poor biomechanics (PB)} = \text{Pain (P)}$$

$$PH + KI + PB = P$$

What if we took away just one item from the left side of the equation? Would the end result still be the same? Most likely the answer is no. Often, pain is the sum total of a series of events in exactly the same way. A little stress here, plus a strain there, plus an inefficient movement carrying slightly too much weight, and pain is the unhappy result. Change anything on the left side of the equation and the answer on the right side is always different. (Your school math teacher was so right!) Instead of looking for the one key which created pain, it is often more productive to look at the whole series of events.

There is a very positive aspect to pain being the confluence of events. The likelihood that one would combine all those particular events again, which would be needed to produce the same outcome, is quite low. I often find myself telling clients (who fear this new pain may happen again) that if they tried to create this pain, they probably could not accomplish it. It took all the pieces to create the result; any piece by itself would not result in pain. Often, this gives them the courage to continue being active, which is usually the best way to ensure that the pain does not return.

Predictability...

Closely related to meaning and context is predictability and fair-warning. If pain happens at an unpredictable rate and sequence, the experience of pain is worse. We prefer experiences that are predictable and we fear that which is random, and pain is no exception.

One example of this is exemplified by Ivan Pavlov and his experiments on dogs. These were far more complex than just conditioning, and Pavlov was astoundingly insightful and his work was utterly amazing. In one of his experiments, he trained the dogs to respond to shocks with salivation, by feeding the dogs after each shock he administered. Therefore, Pavlov changed the meaning of a painful stimulus (shock) to the expectation of coming reward. The meaning of the shock was reinterpreted, which was an amazing insight in itself. If we interpret what is typically perceived as painful as the precursor of coming pleasure, it is not a "painful" stimulus. While Pavlov did this through conditioning, we can also accomplish this through executive functions in our brain by choosing actions that in the short term would seem to be painful, but result in future reward and pleasure.

With Pavlov's experiments, it got even more interesting. The dogs were initially administered the shock each time in exactly the same place on their body. After the meaning of the shock was transformed from pain to the anticipation of something good (dinnertime!), Pavlov began to change the exact location of the shock. If the subsequent shock was very close to the original site, the dog just assumed the meaning was the same as the original shock. The farther away from the original site the electricity was administered, the more confused the animals became about the meaning of the shock. As the meaning became less and less clear, the experiment produced severe stress for the dogs.

The negative effect of randomness is also seen experimentally in current research labs. In studies with laboratory rats, food was given to them at regular intervals and then suddenly randomized (see the Recommended Reading section). The same amount of food, given randomly, was much more stressful than a predictable delivery schedule of food. Similarly, rats who received unpredictable shocks suffered much more from stress and ulcers than rats that had some sense of predictability to the pain.

Past experience, timelines, and meaning

If the brain prefers predictability, order, and clear meaning, it will look to relate the current experience to something in the past that resembles it. A good deal of the function of past experience is to help predict the future course of events. Perceived chronology of pain is extremely important for interpreting the present experience of pain. Again, imagine two scenarios.

> Angie is experiencing pain in her back, which she has never had previously. Although she has been very active lately (moving her elderly parents), she is extremely concerned about this pain. It is quite debilitating and stressful; something she doesn't need in addition to finding out that her sister was recently diagnosed with breast cancer. This is traumatic as Angie is a breast cancer survivor of three years.

Sydney is also experiencing back pain, also after moving her parents out of their home and into an assisted living facility. Sydney has experienced this pain before, most recently after moving her youngest son out of his apartment after finishing college. That pain, due to too much lifting and cleaning, lasted about three days.

Imagine how different the experience of back pain will be for these two people. Sydney believes that this pain will last three to four days, just like the last bout of pain she experienced. The meaning is simple: she carried one too many boxes. Angie could read the meaning of her pain totally differently than would Sydney. The key point is that Angie had cancer three years previously. With her sister's cancer in the forefront of her mind, a major component of Angie's pain experience is her fear that the back pain isn't just from over-exertion—it could signal a metastasis (spreading of her cancer). The pain is possibly a sign of something that could be pervasive and permanent, a worst-case scenario. Angie is suffering in a way that Sydney is not.

Another aspect of meaning and context is exemplified in the after-effects of trauma. While one would think the severity of the post-trauma experience is in linear relationship to the severity of the trauma, this is not always the case.

Being the victim of a non-fatal gunshot would certainly be a terrible trauma. If you or I were wounded while being an innocent bystander in a storefront burglary, the trauma from the gunshot would be devastating. This would likely be followed by very intense pain and suffering. In war, however, getting shot does not always produce this after-effect. The meaning of the trauma (getting shot) in war can be very different from being an innocent bystander wounded in a convenience store robbery. In war, the soldier has done his/her job admirably, sacrificed much, and has possibly earned the right to return to loved ones back home. The trauma (getting shot) could also reflect the effort to save someone's life in the line of duty. The after-effect of being shot while saving the life of a fellow soldier is very different from the meaningless suffering produced by being shot during a robbery or being the victim of an errant gunshot in a drive-by shooting. It isn't just the event or trauma; it is the meaning of the event.

In addition to the meaning attached to the event, when that meaning is assigned also seems to be important. If at all possible, meaning assigned pre-event has a much better outcome than meaning assigned after the event. In our previous examples, our soldier knew he/she was in danger. Our victim of a drive-by shooter wakes up in a hospital, and must assign the context (and thus meaning) of the trauma after the event.

The difference in outcomes from pre-event and post-event meaning assignment is also exemplified in car accidents involving whiplash. Imagine again two scenarios:

> You are sitting at a light, waiting patiently for it to change. As your mind wanders from tasks needing to be accomplished at work to plans for your daughter's birthday party, the unmistakable sound of screeching brakes fill the air. Glancing at the mirror, you realize the sound is from the car behind you. Seeing this car is not going to stop in time, you brace and look at the car in front of you, hoping that there is enough space for your car to skid to a stop before it smashes into that car too.

> You are sitting at a light, waiting patiently for it to change. As your mind wanders from the tasks needing to be accomplished at work to plans for your daughter's birthday party, suddenly you are hurled forward from a powerful impact. No warning, no nothing, just a sudden jolt.

Your nervous system will respond very differently to those two events. First, let's assume that the physics are exactly the same—the speed, direction, and other criteria are all identical. Second, the recipient is the same in both circumstances with all the same physical characteristics. Neurologist Robert Scaer has studied this extensively and has postulated some interesting concepts on how the brain, specifically a part of the brain called the amygdala, processes such events (Scaer 2001). As you might have guessed, the difference lies in the meaning the brain assigns to these physical events, not the events themselves.

Who do you think will fare better in our whiplash scenario, the person who knew the accident was going to happen or the person who was unaware? Which person could more clearly understand the meaning of the stimuli? The person who was aware of the impending crash understood what the sights and sounds meant; his/her brain did not have to guess. The unaware person had to assign meaning to the sensory data *after* the fact. The long-term outcomes of retrofitting meaning are not very good. It is much preferable to be aware of the crash—although it is not likely you will get a choice in the matter!

Many people struggle with this concept as it conflicts with the idea that a drunk driver will survive a crash better than someone who is sober. Whiplash accidents are completed in less than one second, while many accidents caused by drunk drivers are multi-second events. It may be true that in a multi-second accident, being relaxed is helpful. In a one-second crash, being unaware and completely relaxed leads to injuries that are far worse.

To understand this how this process works, we need to review the function of the amygdala. This part of the brain processes sensory data and evaluates the meaning and emotional content. As meaning is often an aspect of memory (we compare the present experience with a similar past experience and then derive possible meaning), the amygdala often works closely with the hippocampus, the part of the brain that deals with memory.

During the impact, the nervous system is flooded with a massive input of sensory data to the thalamus and the amygdala. At the point of trauma, sensory information and acquisition is amazingly heightened. Imagine being chased by an armed escaped convict while you were hiking in the woods. Hiding behind a tree, I'd bet you could hear the snap of a twig at 50 yards, something you probably could not do during normal functioning. This is due to the release of norepinephrine and epinephrine into the bloodstream, which prepares the body/brain for possible attack. Memory is enhanced, alertness increases, and blood is diverted to skeletal muscle so that quick action can be taken. The amygdala then communicates with the hippocampus, the part of the brain where memory is centered. The hippocampus then searches the archives for a past experience that sheds a possible light on the present circumstances.

Once, while I was giving a lecture on pain mechanisms, a banquet table was dropped by the setup staff in the next conference room. One of my participants seemingly jumped out of his skin, while the rest of us were merely startled. His reaction scared my group more than the sound of the falling table next door. Apologizing for his outburst, he explained that he had just returned from Iraq, where he had served two terms of duty. In Iraq, improvised explosive devices are a very common cause of death for the soldiers and are much feared.

This young man was willing to share with the group how the experience in Iraq had affected him. When he hears loud sounds, his brain takes him right back to the battlefield. His response is more than an exaggerated startle reflex, something that all of us experience when hearing a loud unexpected noise. In his case, the noise is immediately followed by the taste and smell of the desert sand while he reaches for a weapon that is no longer there. His brain has bound an unexpected loud noise to certain tastes, smells, body actions, and responses. The sound triggers his body to reach for his gun and take cover.

The noise is not a merely a stimulus for creating a predicted reaction, just the same as a specific physical experience does not always lead to a predictable pain response. Everyone in that room heard the same noise but only one person reacted so violently. The severity of his reaction was due to his perceived potential meaning of the noise. For the rest of us, the noise had no meaning other than mere surprise. For this young man, the meaning of a sudden loud outburst is that his life is being threatened.

Similarly, I also know a man who was shot down in a helicopter over an area of battle where you really don't want to be stranded (not that getting shot down anywhere is a good thing). Spinning out of control, his helicopter hurtled towards the ground. On the way down, diesel fuel from a bullet to the fuel tank sprayed onto him. To this day, when he smells diesel fuel, he is right back in Vietnam, his pulse racing and his nervous system on edge, feeling as though he is in that helicopter once again. (Obviously, he will never purchase a diesel car.)

The important point is that pain isn't merely the experience of a massive level of negative sensations, with more being worse. The severity of pain can be more dependent on the meaning of the stimulus experienced than the amount. A low-level pain with no known cause that persists for months can be far more devastating than a pain that is intense and linked to a specific and known cause. Perhaps this is true because if the cause is known, one can seek not to repeat the event. This, of course, links to the perception of control. The moment the injury happens *to* you instead of being something you choose, control is lost. With loss of control comes an increase in the experience of pain. Similarly, when the meaning of pain is clear and has a predictable timeline, the pain experience is lessened.

CHAPTER 7

ATTENTION AND PAIN
Gorilla? What gorilla?

"I have had bouts of pain before, but this one really got my attention."

Statements like the one above hold the essence of the mystery of pain and attention. Somehow, we intuitively know that attention and pain are inextricably linked. While we know that pain can capture our attention, does it automatically follow that a lack of attention to pain will result in less discomfort? Does attention to pain itself always increase the pain experience?

In reality, attention can be used to increase or decrease pain, depending on how attention is used. This can be confusing to both practitioner and patient alike. Attention is like a knife that can be incredibly useful and dangerous at the same time: a tool to reduce pain or an experience that can make pain much worse. My hope is to clarify this process and make the power of attention work to diminish your experience of pain.

First, we should explore what attention is. Attention is the power of focus, the ability to direct where the mind places the beam of its searchlight. The light of attention highlights everything in the path of the beam and diminishes everything outside its path. Attention isn't something that happens to you—in fact, you get to direct the game plan. Scientists would call this "executive control." Research has revealed that the brain regions activated during activities requiring attention are the superior frontal, inferior parietal, and superior temporal cortex. These areas of the brain deal with self-awareness, sensory processing, and sensorimotor integration. The cortex is the part of your brain that deals with the "thinking" you. The mid-brain, also known as the lower brain, deals with the affective or emotional aspects of pain.

Various parts of the human nervous system deal with stimuli quite differently. One model of thinking about these regions of the brain is a concept known as the triune brain, a theory of brain development proposed by Paul MacLean (1990), an American neuroscientist.

In this model of brain development, the oldest part of our brain is the reptilian brain. The reptilian brain controls functions such as body temperature, heart rate, breathing, and essentially involuntary body actions. The reptilian brain reacts reflexively, before thinking or emotion take place. When you jerk your hand away from a sharp object, action precedes thought. If you had to wait for thought to create the appropriate action, it may be too late. The motto for the reptilian brain is act first, think later.

The Paleomammalian brain (the mid-brain, sometimes referred to as the limbic brain) is the emotional center of the brain. The areas of the limbic system include the amygdala, hippocampus, and cingulate cortex, all structures known to play a very large role in pain perception. The connection between pain and emotions is very important; pain is thought to be as much an emotional experience as a purely sensory experience.

Last, the Neomammalian brain (neocortex) of our brain houses the capacity for cognition, our capability for abstract thought and planning—essentially, our ability to think. Cognition can be a very valuable tool for combating pain when used appropriately. For example, if I described the following physical sensations: quickened pulse, faster breathing, heightened alertness, what might you imagine you are experiencing? These are the physical sensations of fear, but they are also present when you are excited and anticipating something pleasant to unfold. Similarly, if you are a violinist about to play a concert, having your thinking brain re-label what you feel as excitement, not fear, could be the difference between success and failure. On the other hand, cognition out of control (imagining disasters that haven't yet occurred) can lead us into more pain. (I think, therefore I hurt?)

There is ample evidence that the brain regions of the neocortex and the mid-brain seem to counteract each other: when the higher brain (neocortex) activates, mid-brain activity decreases. Perhaps attention can be thought of as a zero sum game: there is only so much mental energy available at any one time. The theory regarding attention and pain is that if attention activates the neocortex (thinking brain) which then inhibits mid-brain (emotional) activation, pain should decrease since the mid-brain area is highly involved in pain. Thus, the more you direct your brain power to being completely cognitively engaged, the less activated the emotional centers of the brain become.

While there is ample evidence to support this idea, research efforts in attention suffer from a confounding variable: the ability to mentally focus is a skill which varies widely from person to person. In research environments, the researchers never quite know if a failure of attention to diminish pain is because attention does not diminish pain or whether the subject was unable to sustain mental focus. This affects both the research environment and also our own experience with attention and pain. The more capable you are at concentrating and sustaining focus, the more powerful the effect of attention can be. This is also perhaps the reason why attention seems to be more effective in dealing with lower intensity pain, rather than high-level pain. The more intense the pain, the more likely it is to win the attention game.

One of the most striking examples of selective attention is revealed in a video created by Dr. Daniel Simons. This video explores selective attention through visual awareness and illustrates this concept masterfully. In one of the videos, Dr. Simons has a group of students tossing a basketball to each other. There are two groups of students, one team wearing white shirts and the other group wearing black shirts. Each is tossing a basketball to members of his own team. The white-shirted and black-shirted teams are co-mingling, weaving around each other. Before playing the video, the viewers are asked to count the number of times the white-shirted team passes the ball to each other. In order to do this, the viewer must also ignore visual information coming from the black-shirted team, since this is non-essential to the assigned task. I find it interesting that when I play this for a large group of people, the number of passes reported is widely variable. If we are all watching the same video, why do we get such a wide range in numbers?

More interestingly, in the middle of the video, a student in a black gorilla suit walks on to the screen, pounds his/her chest, and slowly walks off. The majority of people viewing the video never see the gorilla. When I make them view it again, with no assigned task (counting passes), these people swear I have switched videos as some sort of trick. Since the gorilla is in a black suit and the instructions are to concentrate on the white-shirted team, all information regarding black data is deselected, including the gorilla. Attention is selective. You may wish to read Dr. Simons' excellent book, *The Invisible Gorilla* (Chabris and Simons 2010).

The power of attention involves both the ability to focus on the desired data and the ability to deselect all non-essential stimuli. It is perhaps the second task of deselection that is far more difficult than the first. I sit down to write this book, yet I am aware of the need to attend to a myriad of other tasks that pull at my attention. All of these other tasks have merit, but none of them will help me accomplish the goal of finishing this book. What we call the ability to focus is largely the ability to exclude non-essential data. (I remember Clara, one of my mentors, telling me that she doubted my ability to finish this book. She said I was too nice, not ruthless enough with the decisions I make about my time. At the time, I really did not understand her words and thought them needlessly harsh. In the midst of writing this book, the necessity to cut other stimuli from my life brought her words to the forefront. As anyone who has done a similar project knows, writing exacts a high price. Often, that price is paid largely by the family of the writer. As you are reading these words, I must have learned some measure of ruthlessness and selectivity. I am pretty sure that this is what Clara intended in the first place.)

In our gorilla suit/basketball video, the visual cortex is bombarded with data from the screen. One would think that we simply see what is on the screen. Alas, this is not so. We do not see what is there; we see what we pay attention to, which is filtered through the lens of perception. Data is constantly flooding our system and our brains cannot process all of it; we need filters to sort out non-relevant data. How do we accomplish this selective attention and what does that mean for the experience of pain? If attention is a competition, who wins?

This question has perplexed scientists for many years and there are some recent insights into the process. One eminent researcher, Professor Robert Desimone (Bichot, Rossi, and Desimone 2005), has given us some insight into the filtering capabilities of the mind. His research into visual processing shows that when neurons synchronize, they command our attention because the force of the signal is now stronger. His research delves into the V4 area of the brain, which is the area of attention with regard to visual processing. If you are looking for a specific image, like viewing a painting that has a face hidden inside the image, do you scan the painting in an organized grid until you see the image? Or is it better to step back a bit and just let the image appear out of the chaos? How do we know when we first see the face?

The answer seems to be that when the neurons that are preferential to what we are looking for fire, they fire first as individual neurons. As more of these neurons begin to fire, the individual neurons start to synchronize with each other, creating a stronger voice. Imagine a group of friends hunting for Morel mushrooms in a large wooded area. Soon, isolated individuals call out "found one." If successful individuals are all calling out separately, it is hard for the unsuccessful searchers to hear the successful exclamations over the din of their conversation. But if all the successful hunters start calling out in unison, the power of their calls will be noticed above all other stimuli.

In the mystery of pain, neurons that are preferential to the data *we are looking for* probably get our attention first, just like in Desimone's studies. The gorilla video exemplifies two important points. First, *what you look for, you find*. If you expect something to be painful it will be. Second, *attention focused away from pain can decrease our experience of discomfort* through distraction. Let's explore expectation first.

Pain and expectation

Expectation is a powerful way to sort through the volumes of data that constantly bombard our brains every day. With regard to the gorilla video referred to earlier, if I had instructed you to look for a gorilla on the video, you would have seen it. Had I told you to count the number of times the black-shirted team passed the ball, your likelihood of seeing the black-suited gorilla would have been substantially higher since you would be looking for something black. This point is fascinating; when you look for data (such as a movement) that also is tied to a color (in this case white), the neurons that fire in response to color are preferentially excited and will notice the particular color more quickly. In our gorilla video, the fact that people were concentrating on white-shirted players helps exclude the black-shirted players. What we look for we see, what we are not looking for we ignore.

Let's apply selective attention with regard to pain. Some very interesting studies have been done in Japan that looked at changes in the brain, specifically the anterior cingulate cortex (ACC) and the region including parietal operculum and posterior insula (PO/PI), during the expectation of pain. These studies reveal fascinating insights into how the brain anticipates pain and reinterprets normal stimuli as potentially noxious.

In one study (Sawamoto *et al.* 2000), the researchers used a laser to create heat on the back of the receiving subjects' hands. The level of heat produced by the laser could range from warm to painfully hot. The subjects were given careful instructions about two aspects of the heat sensation, intensity and unpleasantness. Like volume on a radio, these two sensations can be different. The massive sound of a complete symphony orchestra can be very intense, but not unpleasant. As the volume level goes up, at some point the volume transitions from intense to unpleasant. Once the subjects knew how to score the sensations, and each individual's pain tolerance was calibrated, the researchers began.

In one session, the subjects were given 20 laser stimulations that were about 160–200 percent of their pain tolerance and 20 laser stimulations that were simply a non-painful warm stimulus. These stimulations were randomized so the subjects never knew whether the next stimulation was going to be painful or non-painful. In another session, subjects were given only 20 non-painful stimulations and they were certain that these stimulations would be non-painful.

In essence, there were three experiences. There was a painful stimulus experience, a non-painful stimulation the subject did not know was coming, and a non-painful stimulus the subject knew was going to be non-painful.

Not surprisingly, the painful stimulus was experienced as very unpleasant to the subjects. What is more interesting is how the subjects responded to the non-painful stimuli. In the session where they expected only non-painful warmth, they rated the experience very low on the unpleasant scale. In the session where painful and non-painful were randomized (therefore the subject did not know which was coming next), the non-painful warmth was rated much more unpleasant.

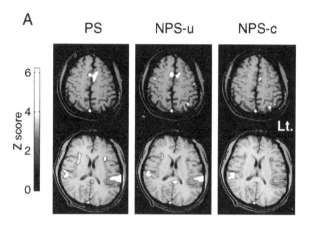

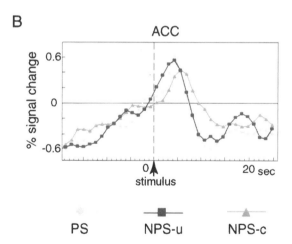

Figure 7.1: In this fMRI image, notice how similar the PS (Painful Stimulus) and NPS-u (Non-Painful Stimulus-uncertain) look. Compare that to the image at the far right, NPS-c (Non-Painful Stimulus-certain) where the subject knew the coming stimulus was not painful.

The way this study was organized essentially eliminated the possibility of other variables causing the increase in pain. The difference was the uncertainty of the strength of the next stimulus. Even when the laser was set on low, the warmth produced was still deemed unpleasant. This is the key: the subjects realized during the stimulation whether the intensity was high or low, but they still perceived the non-painful stimulus as unpleasant, regardless of the intensity of the stimulus.

While this experiment was happening, the researchers were also using a special type of MRI called functional magnetic resonance imaging (fMRI) on specific structures in the brain, the anterior cingulate cortex (ACC), and the region including parietal operculum and posterior insula (PO/PI). (An fMRI is a very special type of MRI that monitors brain activity through blood flow. Scientists can observe activity in the brain at the moment it happens.) The fMRI scans did show activation in all of these expected areas during the application of the painful stimulus. What is truly remarkable is the result of the fMRI scans of subjects during the non-painful stimulus. When the stimuli were randomized so the subjects did not know which one was coming, the scans of the non-painful stimuli looked just like the painful stimuli scans. One can barely tell them apart.

In a similar experiment, Dr. Howard Fields used visual clues to pair with the heat stimulus (Keltner *et al.* 2006). The researchers first paired the color blue with a mild heat sensation to the back of the hand. When subjects were given intense heat to the back of the hand, it was paired with the color red. The subjects were then put in an fMRI machine and the experiment continued. This time, if the subjects saw the color blue (previously shown paired with a mild stimulus) before an intense stimulus, they rated the discomfort lower. Conversely, if they saw the color red before a mild stimulus, they rated the intensity and unpleasantness higher. Pairing the mild stimulus with the blue color produced the least pain, while pairing the intense stimulus with the color red produced the most discomfort.

The implications of these experiments are astounding. When people do not know what to expect and a previous stimulus has been painful, the brain will respond to the next stimulus as if it too was painful. This is true in spite of the fact that the subjects state that the stimulus is less intense than the previous stimulus. (Remember, the subjects often said that the stimulus was less on the intensity scale but significant on the unpleasantness scale.) This is the same stimulus that the subjects said was low on intensity and unpleasantness when all the non-painful stimuli were grouped together and expected. As we have seen in other areas, the experience of pain is not a singular event; it affects the interpretation and experience of *future* events. This is why pain must not be allowed to linger indefinitely; it may make the experience of future pain more likely. (In an interesting note, pain can also color the past. If researchers ask subjects about their past pain, the report will be substantially influenced by the current pain state. If the subject is currently in pain, he/she will rate past history of pain as being higher than if the current pain level is low.)

Pain and thinking about pain

As mentioned earlier, activation of the neocortex is typically associated with a decrease in activity in the mid-brain region and therefore less pain. This *should* make cognition the antidote to pain. However, the shadow side of cognition is that we can also think ourselves into pain as easily as we can think ourselves out of it. As with so many aspects of our brain, the sword cuts both ways. Let's explore the negative aspect of imagery first.

As we currently understand, rabbits do not lie awake worrying about whether the shoulder pain they feel is due to arthritic changes, a ligament injury, or some serious degenerative disorder. We humans, however, can drive ourselves completely crazy with the thoughts we create in our imagination. Our thinking brain can help us lessen pain or drive us absolutely crazy; we get to choose, but the choosing isn't easy.

Dread: I can't stop myself

The presence of dread can substantially increase the experience of pain. While you may assume dread is a type of fear, it is slightly different from fear and is processed in a different part of the brain. Fear is processed largely in the amygdala and is emotionally driven, while dread seems to be much more aligned with the experience of attention than the emotion of fear. When you can't stop thinking about a possible future negative event, that is dread. Fear may involve very little thinking; it is primarily an emotional experience.

How does dread play into the experience of pain? Let's take the example of the person who suffers back pain on a frequent basis. When the back is doing well, it is hard to completely enjoy any respite from pain. When chronic back pain sufferers experience a pain-free period, they typically increase activity levels. At some point, they will often begin to fear whether or not the increased activity will have negative consequences. The brain scans the body for telltale signs of impending spasm, which the person assumes is sure to come after too much activity. What you look for, you generally find. Is the subsequent back pain a product of the increased activity or a result of the mind's expectation of pain?

This self-prophecy is similar to the golfer who shoots a 43 on the front nine of a difficult golf course. If this golfer normally shoots in the mid-90s, he/she will frequently score much worse on the back nine, thus making the final score much closer to the normal score. Was the final score reflective of that person's ability or is it reflective of limits placed upon performance via the mind's perception of ability?

In the experience of episodic pain, dread of the consequences of activity is always looming. There is an increased sensitivity to any stimuli, often resulting in a misinterpretation of otherwise innocuous data. Think back to our example of the golfer. After a slightly errant shot on the front nine, the golfer might shrug his/her shoulders and proceed to execute the second shot perfectly. On the back nine, mindful that he/she is playing far better than usual, an errant shot is interpreted as the beginning of impending collapse. The following shot is then loaded with new meaning: mess this up and it's the beginning of a downhill slide.

Dread is the anticipation of a future painful event and the anticipation is often as disconcerting as the dreaded event itself. We all know this from our personal experience of putting off doing our taxes, cleaning the basement, getting that colonoscopy, or going to the dentist. When we put our attention into the future experience, we experience dread and dread increases pain.

The effect of dread was shown in a very clever study by Dr. Gregory Berns (Berns *et al.* 2006). The dread itself is as devastating as the pain.

In Berns' study, researchers took 32 subjects and put them in an fMRI scanner to monitor brain activity. The researchers gave the subjects very uncomfortable low-voltage shocks to the foot, 96 times, with varying frequency and intensity. During this process, each subject had his/her maximum tolerance established (how much electricity they could stand). Once this tolerance was established, the subjects were informed that never would the baseline maximum tolerance be repeated, but the shocks they would experience were either 10, 30, 60, or 90 percent of that maximum value. Additionally, subjects were informed that these shocks could come at delays of 1, 3, 9, or 27 seconds.

After establishing this baseline, subjects were given some interesting choices. Various combinations of time delay and amount of shock were offered to the subjects, 36 combinations in all. The subject might be offered a 30 percent shock in 27 seconds or a 60 percent shock in nine seconds. Of the 32 subjects in the group, 23 of them had a perfectly rational response to pain. They were termed the "mild dreaders": these people would choose to get the shock out of the way quickly, as long as the shock was not significantly greater than the delayed shock. These people took the shock/pain on their terms by choosing the time. Other people in the group, termed "extreme dreaders," would rather experience a shock immediately, even if the immediate shock was much greater than the one coming later. For these people, waiting for a lesser shock was more unpleasant than experiencing a greater shock immediately.

That some people would choose to "get it over with" quickly is perhaps not so remarkable in light of our own personal experiences. This attitude can be a really functional approach to unpleasant tasks. Some people would just rather tackle the tough job right away and get it behind them. On the other hand, immediacy can also be a problem. Imagine a person at a cocktail party who senses that his/her spouse is displeased with a comment or action. The "dreader" would probably be much wiser to delay addressing this conflict until later in private, perhaps on the way home. However, for a "dreader," the delay is too painful so he/she will try to address the situation immediately, with unfortunate social consequences. Interestingly, the "dreader" does not think of the social consequences because he/she is too consumed with the internal conflict to consider the external circumstances.

Using attention to decrease pain

As we have just explored, attention can be used to increase the experience of pain. On the other hand, there are many ways that directed attention can decrease pain. Many of these are easy to employ and are quite effective.

Directing attention from the top down

Top-down processing is to use the cognitive, thinking brain, to override the feeling brain. The really valuable example of top-down processing is to focus the mind on various specific details of the pain experience, rather than its emotional component (mid-brain), which can lead to more pain. This form of attention can be valuable in cases where the person has chronic pain and has the ability to focus on specific aspects of that pain experience. While the cognitive brain is engaged in calibrating and quantifying the experience, activation of the emotional brain decreases.

Just recently, one of my clients underwent an MRI. She was quite surprised at how scary it was for her; the tight quarters caused her to feel claustrophobic and the sound was much louder than she expected. Her heart began to race and she began to suffer a panic attack. Cleverly, she began to draw on her expertise as a drummer. She began listening closely for rhythmic patterns in the sounds, establishing patterns and phrasing. When she mentally tired of analyzing the sounds, she began imagining intricate movement patterns with her fingers. Soon, the entire MRI was completed without incident.

I have seen top-down processing of the pain experience cleverly employed by experienced pain management nurses. They often encourage a patient to answer such questions as:

- If your pain was a color, what color would it be?

- If it was a sound, what kind of sound would it be?

- If your pain had a face, could you draw it for me?

- If it was a surface, what kind of surface would it be?

I do not mean to suggest that bottom-up processing is always to be ignored or inhibited. There are times when our primary responses are enormously valuable, just as there are times when they can be very misleading.

An example of a misleading bottom-up response is the following. Mary is at a restaurant, having a wonderful time talking to her friends. Suddenly, she has difficulty breathing and her body is extremely tense. She can sense that she is on full alert but is clueless as to the reason. Gradually she realizes the source of her unease. There is a man at this restaurant that looks exactly like someone who assaulted her many years ago. She absolutely knows that this man is not that person, but the resemblance is remarkable.

In this example, the body also has a mind of its own. Mary knows that the man at the restaurant is not her attacker, but she cannot stop her body from feeling the way it does. Telling herself to calm down is only managing the situation after the fear has already surfaced. How will Mary stop herself from going into fear mode whenever she sees anyone who resembles her attacker?

It is the essence of sensorimotor psychotherapy to approach this dilemma from both directions. From the book *Trauma and the Body*, consider the following:

> In sensorimotor psychotherapy, top-down direction is harnessed to support sensorimotor processing rather than just to manage it. The client might be asked to mindfully track (a top-down cognitive process) the sequence of physical sensations and impulses (sensorimotor process) as they progress through the body, and to temporarily disregard emotions and thoughts that arise, until the bodily sensations and impulses resolve to a point of rest and stabilization. (Ogden, Minton, and Pain 2006)

I have seen many people use the principles of sensorimotor psychotherapy quite successfully. It is certainly preferable to have a therapist who is trained in these principles guide you through the process.

Meditation

There are also two approaches to meditation that apply similar top-down approaches to pain modulation. One approach, Focused Attention, is much like distraction. It works by concentrating the mind on one single stimulus to the exclusion of all others. The other, Open Presence, takes the opposite approach, which is not to focus on anything at all, only to observe that which passes in front of the mind with a spirit of detachment. The desired state of awareness is to experience stimuli without any emotional reaction. Dispassion is the key to keeping the brain from having an emotional reaction and thus interpreting the stimuli as noxious.

A 2009 paper indeed confirmed that meditation is a useful tool in decreasing pain (Grant and Rainville 2009). When they compared experienced meditators with non-meditators, the meditation group had a higher pain tolerance by about 20 percent. This was true whether the meditators were actively meditating or not. The pain source in this instance was intense heat applied to the lower leg (researchers seem to like this method a lot!). A computer-controlled heating plate varied from 43 degrees Celsius to a maximum of 53 degrees Celsius. Many in the meditator group tolerated the maximum temperature, while none of the control (non-meditator) group did. As the temperature increased, researchers noticed that the meditation group slowed their breathing rate (breaths per minute) in response to the temperature increase to a rate that was 20 percent less than the non-meditator group.

Distraction as pain relief

In the attention game, the opposite of focus towards the pain experience is distraction away from the area of pain. Is distraction a useful tool for pain relief?

The answer to that question is affirmative, as many of us have experienced in one form or another. As we have seen before, attention is selective. Direct the mind to one area and you do so to the exclusion of another stimulus. If you are absorbed in listening to Bach's Goldberg Variations, you may not hear your spouse calling you. Focus on winning a grueling chess match and you may not feel your rear end pleading to get up out of the chair. Our daily experience supports this idea, but does it hold up in the research environment?

In a clever experiment, Susanna Bantick and her colleagues used fMRI scanning to explore that question more deeply (Bantick *et al.* 2002). As the method of distraction, the subjects were given a task called the Counting Stroop Test. The Counting Stroop Test is a fascinating and deceptively difficult little task. Subjects are given a visual field that contains a random number of simple words repeated. They are told to press a button to indicate how many times the word shows up in the box. For example, here the subject would push a button for the number three, as the word Beagle was shown three times:

Beagle
Beagle
Beagle

To create a context where attention was increased because of the complexity of the task, the researchers added an interference factor. In addition to the original box of words, the researchers added boxes that listed the names of numbers. The interference box might look like the following:

Two
Two
Two

Although the subjects were instructed to count down the number of times the word appears, the temptation is to push the button for the number two, since that is what you are reading on the screen. To override this inclination takes a substantial amount of concentration. The researchers hypothesized that the amount of mental energy devoted to accomplishing this task could be used as a distraction for pain.

To test the effect of distraction and pain, the researchers used heat stimulation (50–53.5 degrees Celcius) on the hand to produce the experience of pain. The subjects were exposed to the heat stimulation while executing the simple counting task (no number interference) and also with the number interference (boxes with names of numbers that did not add up to the numbers). What Bantick found was not surprising: the experience of pain was normal when the subjects were given the simple counting task with no number interference. When the subjects were given the number interference and therefore had to concentrate more intensely to get the right answer, the experience of pain was much less. This was confirmed both by the subject's subjective scoring and also by the fMRI data of the anterior cingulate cortex and the insula. Attention directed away from pain will decrease the experience of pain.

Guidelines for directing attention away from pain

Here are a few guidelines that can help make distraction a more effective approach in managing pain:

- *Preselection.* If you have pain and wish to use selective attention to counter it, selecting what you wish to focus on is crucial. Put on a piece of classical music and decide that you will follow only the cello part for as long as you can. Watch a football game and pay attention only to the offensive line, not where the football is thrown. In whatever activity you choose, only focus on a single aspect of the total event. This focus will command your attention and deselect the pain experience.

- *Novelty.* Put yourself in an environment that is new for you, such as learning a new activity. The more compelling due to unfamiliarity, the better. For instance, if you have never danced before, consider taking classes in swing, ballroom, salsa, or whatever dance might appeal to you. Get your spouse involved. Learn a video game, take piano lessons, or learn to crochet. Whatever it is, you must be interested in it and it must be new to you. Once you master it, keep challenging yourself.

- *Signal strength.* Whatever activity you choose, immerse your whole brain into it. Passively watching a game or mechanically going over your piano lessons is not going to generate enough brainpower to negate the pain you are experiencing. Find a way to make the activity as compelling as possible.

- *Link with emotion.* Link the new stimuli with an emotional experience. If you are taking piano lessons, link the learning with the reason for that intense desire to play the piano. Perhaps you always wanted to play for your son's wedding or for a surprise at your mom's birthday party. Whatever the reason, linking the learning to an emotionally compelling reason increases attention. Choose the activity based on your intense emotional reason to do it, not because you think you should.

Whether you choose to focus on aspects and qualities of the pain (focused attention) or direct your attention away from pain (distraction), the key to success seems to be complete and total focus. Half-hearted attempts or the inability to direct attention completely will probably result in failure. To illustrate this concept, allow me to describe a very clever experiment that can teach us a very important lesson about attention.

If you are learning a new skill, your brain is changing in response to new demands. The ability for your brain to undergo constant change is called neural plasticity and is the subject of an enormous body of research (see the Recommended Reading section). Using fMRI scans, it is now possible to see the changes in the brain that occur in response to these new demands. For example, let's say that this new skill acquisition is learning to play the cello. Since I would be fingering the cello with my left hand, the motor area in the right side of my brain that controls my left hand would grow and change in response to new demands. These changes would then be visible on an MRI scan in just two weeks.

In the laboratory, it is also possible to do the same thing (strengthen a primate's corresponding motor area of the brain) by using very mild electric shocks to the animal's digits. Since the animal does not understand electricity, the animal's attention is directed to this strange sensation (mild shock) that keeps happening in his digits. If this is done daily, just like practicing the cello daily, the motor map of the primate's brain connected to the left hand will grow significantly. This has been demonstrated many times, but researchers Gregg Recanzone and William Jenkins took the research one step further (Schwartz and Begley 2002).

Recanzone and Jenkins not only applied mild shocks to the digits, but simultaneously trained the animals to listen for changes in sound. The animals were conditioned that when the sound changes, food will follow. In these experiments, the shocks to the left digits had essentially no effect on the motor map on the right side of the brain. Why? The animal's attention was focused on the change in sound, because that is where the food was. Just having a stimulus present is not enough; directed attention to the presenting stimulus is the key.

Merzenich (Recanson, Schreiner, and Merzenich 1993) did exactly the opposite, but showed exactly the same effect. In this study, the animals were trained to pay attention to very specific sounds. As long as the animals were learning to discern the differences in sound frequencies, the part of the brain that processes sound (the auditory cortex) underwent changes and reorganization. When the researchers distracted the animals from the primary task of listening to the sound frequencies, the auditory cortex underwent little if any change.

This is a significant lesson for all of us. I always think about these experiments when I watch someone mechanically go through the motions in an exercise program. Are they really getting maximal neural benefit from their workout? I am sure there is some value, certainly cardiac benefits, but I think the benefit to the whole brain would be greater if attention was directed to the activity rather than to the TV screen in front of them.

While distraction can be a very functional approach to pain management, some studies show it to be most effective when dealing with children in pain. In one study at least, distraction seems of less value in reducing pain than focused attention to the athletic activity, described previously as a top-down processing model.

In a study of élite athletes, Dr. John S. Raglin has discovered that intense focus on the activity itself, rather than a distraction, increases performance (Kolata 2010). The downside of distraction is that over time, or at a certain level of intensity, the distraction is overcome by the pain. If attention is on the pain itself, micro-analyzing details of the experience, the person is less likely to be worn down. Dr. Raglin's research teaches us that attention can be an extremely effective way to reduce pain if the focus is on examining aspects of the qualities of the pain experience.

There could be a valuable lesson in his research, translating it to people in chronic pain. The difference in sport, and this is a major difference, is that the pain the athletes endure is volitional. However severe, and riding in the Tour de France is really severe pain, it is pain the riders choose to experience. Getting hit by a car or having lupus is a different story. Pain from the accident or lupus is inflicted upon you, not something you choose to experience. Even with this glaring difference between volitional and non-volitional pain, there are still perhaps principles that can be applied to the experience of chronic pain. Raglin's research teaches us that attention can be an extremely effective way to reduce pain if the focus is on examining aspects of the qualities of the pain experience.

Positive expectation

We have previously examined several instances where negative expectation has led to a substantial increase in the experience of pain. It follows that positive expectations could lead to a decrease in the pain experience.

In one study, researchers explored the role of the expectation of pleasure to decrease pain. Dunn and Herz (Fields 2009) fed rats on a metal plate. This plate was kept at room temperature and two groups of rats were fed. One group got regular food and the other group was fed chocolate-covered biscuits. After conditioning the rats to the food, the researchers heated up the metal plate to uncomfortable temperatures. The researchers sought to explore how much discomfort the rats would endure to get food. As you might expect, rats who were used to getting the chocolate-covered biscuits were willing to stay on the hot plate twice as long as the other rats. The expectation of pleasure (chocolate!) was an analgesic to pain. When the rats who were expecting chocolate were given a drug that blocks the production of endorphins (an opioid substance produced by the body), they no longer were willing to accept more heat than the rats being fed regular food. It seems that chocolate is indeed a great motivator!

Positive imagery and pain

There are many examples of the use of imagery for pain reduction. Imagery can be a strategy by itself or used in conjunction with other techniques such as hypnosis. A friend of mine who is an anesthetist uses hypnosis very effectively to help people in pain. There is fairly solid research that hypnosis can be quite effective in pain control (see the Recommended Reading section). Many of the effective hypnotic techniques utilize visualization techniques, imagining a desired effect or situation vividly. Hypnosis isn't the only way to use such a technique, however.

In a Seattle hospital, there is a burn unit that has been using a video called "Snowworld" to help burn survivors deal with pain while their dressings are changed. Viewing this video has been shown to be very helpful in diminishing pain. One might think that the effectiveness of these viewings would diminish over time, but this has not been shown to be true.

In one of the research studies conducted by my institute, the role of motor imagery (imaginary movement) and restricted neck rotation was explored. People with restricted range were shown a video of a dancer with phenomenal neck range of motion. After watching the dancer move her neck with complete freedom for approximately four minutes, the subjects experienced significant range of motion increases. Thus, what we watch causes our body (through mirror neurons) to respond as if it were actually doing the action; just as what we vividly imagine causes us to experience it as though it was actually happening. Your body cannot tell the real experience from the vividly imagined experience.

In summary, attention is a powerful force that can relieve or worsen our experience of pain. Knowing how and where to direct attention makes all the difference.

CHAPTER 8

FEAR AND PAIN

Be afraid. Be very afraid of being afraid

Fear can play an enormous role in the experience of pain. As we discovered in the IASP definition of pain, *pain is an unpleasant sensory and emotional experience associated with actual or potential tissue damage.* Fear is involved in this definition of pain in two ways. First, it intensifies the emotional experience of the feelings that accompany pain; and second, fear plays a role in the "potential" damage aspect of pain. The fear arises from the possibility that this pain could be a threat to survival and that threat could be either immediate or in the future.

As fear researcher Joseph LeDoux explores in his writings, fear is a primal system of defensive behaviors. These defensive behaviors are a set of physical and emotional responses in the nervous system, perceived as fear because these sensations are interpreted as such. The debate that LeDoux explores revolves around whether our feeling of fear causes the physical responses or whether the physical experiences (increased heart rate, breathing changes, etc.) produce the feeling of fear. In summary, if a person experiences all the physical attributes associated with fear, the physical experience will produce the emotional experience of fear.

Because fear occurs in animals and in humans, it is much more easily explored than other emotions. What makes humans unique is the fact that we can think ourselves (here we go again) into danger, adding another level of fear that (as we know now) does not exist in animals. A rabbit does not sit in a protected environment and scare himself silly imagining what it would be like if a snake suddenly crawled down his hole. We humans, however, can lie awake at night imagining the worst of events, with the resultant effect on our physiology being very close to what would happen if the event was real.

This brings us to an important distinction, fear vs. anxiety. Fear is the response to a very specific stimulus, such as hearing an unfamiliar noise in your house, one loud enough to awaken you. Anxiety is non-specific. For example, you lie awake, unable to sleep, with no specific reason for why you feel so uneasy. Fear is present tense, a reaction to something happening now, and anxiety is future-based, what may happen at some point down the road. The experience of anxiety is similar to fear, but usually less intense because it is not focused on a specific stimulus. While anxiety may be a less intense experience, it can be even more devastating because of its seemingly endless duration. The negative effects of anxiety stem from keeping the fear response mechanism going for a very long time.

When it comes to fear, it is entirely appropriate to reflect on the landmark research in conditioning by Ivan Pavlov, as described earlier. Fear can be conditioned, that is, a dog can be conditioned to know that a certain action is followed by a shock. (Interestingly, so can flies, fish, and worms.) The essence of this effect is probably survival. If an animal is attacked in a particular area of its territory, remembering the location of the attack is essential to survival. So it is with humans. When certain actions cause pain, we remember. This is very helpful in guiding us to avoid actions that irritate and inflame a wound in the acute stage. Memory becomes a problem when experiences from the past are applied inappropriately to the present, thus perpetuating chronic pain states.

Memory and pain

Remembering situations that could lead to pain makes perfect sense, but why don't these memories slowly diminish and then finally disappear (something scientists term "extinguish") over time? In many cases, such as Post-Traumatic Stress Disorder, the memory doesn't fade, but can worsen with time. Memory often becomes a negative factor in pain syndromes not because we cannot remember, but because we are unable to forget. Past experiences of pain are often quite difficult to relegate to the past; these historical traumas have a way of seeping into and coloring our present experience. Any experience in the present that has qualities resembling a past trauma somehow causes the memory train to "jump the tracks," putting us right back into re-experiencing the old trauma. For more insight, we return to Ivan Pavlov.

Pavlov explored the phenomenon of "spontaneous recovery," the concept that a conditioned response could return again (be reinstated) after it had been extinguished. This effect certainly reflects our personal experience (at least mine!) with old demons. Past wounds that should have healed years ago may resurface again at a time of undue stress. As it turns out, the spontaneous recovery effect demonstrates that these old patterns are never fully erased; they are more likely lying dormant. A period of great stress or an experience similar to the original offending event can make the unpleasant memory resurface when we least expect that to happen. Why doesn't the memory of this particular pain experience gradually extinguish itself since the pathway has not been used for decades?

For further insight, research done by Dr. Gene Robinson is very helpful. Dr. Robinson does research with bees, and one of his studies explored how bees can learn to locate their new hive very quickly and very adeptly (Robinson and Dyer 1993). Dr. Robinson took a bee colony and split the hive in two, taking a queen and establishing a new hive in a different part of the meadow. This simulates the natural process of "swarming," when one colony splits into two. From the original colony, half the bees now lived in a new home, where the bees navigate there by turning right at the oak tree, instead of left as they did previously. Remarkably, the bees learned this new location very quickly. Once they did, they did not get mixed up and fly to the old hive (turning left at the oak tree) by mistake. I am sure many of you have had the experience similar to mine where, when being too tired after a long day at work, I found myself at the driveway of my old house. The bees did not do that (they know this because the bees are marked with little dots of paint. It is amazing what grad students have to do!)

Telling the results of his study to another professor, Dr. Robinson remarked how quickly the bees learned (this guy is really proud of his bees) and how well they forget. His colleague astutely pointed out that it was not clear that the bees forgot anything, they just remembered exceedingly well. Challenged and inspired, Dr. Robinson explored this idea by removing the new hive and queen while the forager bees were gone. Without delay, the now homeless bees from the new hive went right back to the original colony. The neural script was not erased, just written over, like the way we used to record cassette tapes over again without going through the expensive method of truly erasing them. Like those cassettes, the original data was still on the tape, just not immediately accessible. The map of the original colony was still present in the bees' brain; they had no trouble accessing it.

While we can only speculate, there are probably very good reasons for nature not to erase the tape. One, writing over it is certainly less expensive, from an energy point of view. Two, and perhaps more importantly, the brain stores the data. In the future, should the old response ever be needed again it could be generated without starting all over. Who is to say that an action will never again be appropriate? The brain saves the shortcut just in case. (It worked for the bees.)

In the mystery of pain, this can be a source of much consternation. Chronic pain can produce pathways of response that we truly would like to erase, or certainly write over for a very long time. Let's look at examples of both stress and similar environments for resurfacing a memory or neural script.

One of the tricks I learned from strength and conditioning expert Al Vermeil is the value of stress to bring old patterns (in this case, muscle imbalance) to the surface. While my structural assessment of an athlete was elaborate and laborious, his was brilliantly simple. He had the athlete stand with a barbell across his shoulders, as if the player was going to do a squat. With an assistant on each side of the player, the assistants began loading weight plates, one after the other, on the barbell. If one shoulder was carried slightly lower than the other, the stress of the added weight magnified the discrepancy, making the lower shoulder collapse first under the weight. Stress magnifies any imbalance. So it is in life.

In addition to overload, another way to bring back an old pattern is to be in an environment similar to the original onset. In one study, researchers conditioned rats to electric shocks. Moving the rats to a different environment, the researchers extinguished the conditioning so that the rats no longer responded to the stimulus with fear. Interestingly, if the rats were returned to the original environment where the fear conditioning was established, they responded with fear to the original stimulus. Even though the rats had learned not to fear the sound anymore, being in the original environment created spontaneous recovery.

As an example, a few years ago I was driving my car in a quiet neighborhood when another car turned directly in front of me. Luckily, neither I nor the other person was injured, but both cars were seriously damaged. Now, every time I drive past that intersection, my body involuntarily tenses. Interestingly, I rode my bicycle through that intersection recently with absolutely no stress response. It is not just the sight of the intersection; it is the context I am in (car vs. bicycle) that re-enlists the memory.

From an evolutionary standpoint, this makes enormous sense. In the experiment with the rats and the environment, you have to admire how clever the brain is. It says, "Wait a minute, I know this place and in here the sound means pain. I am not fooled..." This is a wonderful mechanism as long as the brain does not apply an inappropriate or inaccurate application of memory. How could memory possibly be inappropriate or inaccurate?

The accuracy of memory and its implications in pain

Most of us believe memory to be an exact replay of past events, not unlike having a video recording of everything that happens to us. We often believe that memories are recorded and then stored in the brain as the events occurred and we are often most sure of the ones that had emotional power and significance. Yet again, while this seems to represent our personal experience, the reality seems to be quite different. Anyone who has ever been at a large family gathering has probably experienced this first hand. Sitting around the table, you may have shared a powerful moment in your early life, something which may have powerfully affected your thinking, personality, or in some way shaped who you are now. Amazingly, when recounting the experience (which everyone else at the table was a part of), they all look at you in amazement and disbelief as they share with you very different accounts of the same event. How could something you so vividly recall (and also something that has been with you so long) be negated by the very people who were part of the experience in the first place?

Let's imagine in our example that the original trauma resulted from something that your mother said; you could easily surmise that she just doesn't want to remember saying something so cruel to you. The problem is, there are six other people at the table who were also present at the original event and you are the only one that remembers your version of the event. The only reasoned approach is to accept that by a vote of six to one, the accuracy of your memory is highly suspect. The likely reality is that your mother made a comment that was slightly harsh, but unremarkable to everyone else in the room at the time. Each time you replayed the scene in your mind over the years, you unknowingly altered the details just a bit. What she said got a bit more pointed with each retelling, your reaction a bit more intense. The more you replayed it, the worse it got. Only when you now compare your memory to the experience of others who were in the room at the time (and who had no emotional stake in the event) do you see how far the accuracy of your memory has strayed.

Memory scientists describe the initial process of memory formation as consolidation. Initially, a memory is a bit fragile, but with a bit of time the data (held at first in temporary storage, like cache memory in a computer system) is thought to be sent to the "hard drive" for final storage. Memories are fragile and malleable during the consolidation process, but quite stable when they are stored. During consolidation, your brain is making connections and setting the meaning and context of the event. Recalling the memory at a later time replays the complex neural circuitry created in the initial event. It would perhaps resemble a code in the brain that that says, "Okay, pull memory #937. He wants to see that one again."

What some recent research evidence suggests (thanks to Karim Nader and others, Nader and Einarsson 2010), is that each time a memory is replayed it is subtly altered. Each time we recall a past memory, we bring it back to the surface where it is subject to the same fragile and malleable forces a new memory is exposed to during the consolidation process. Bringing the memory to the surface, where it is again malleable, is called reconsolidation.

In a way, it resembles pulling up a file on your computer again. I have had the document that was this book on my computer for at least three years. There were times when I simply wanted to review what I had written, reading it after making changes several days previously. Rereading that section, I might also wander into other sections of the book, until I run out of my allotted time. Closing the file, it asks me if I want to save changes. Save changes? I don't remember making any changes. Wait though, what if I corrected a few simple typos that I didn't think much about at the time? If I don't save the file, I will probably miss them later. On the other hand, what if, as I highlighted certain paragraphs for review, I accidentally deleted them? Suddenly, I don't know whether to save or not to save. Like memory, the file is vulnerable when it is brought to the forefront and interacted with, not when it is in storage. It is important to remember that research into reconsolidation is in the early stages, but it raises some very important issues with regard to the accuracy of our memories of past pain.

In our earlier scenario involving the family dinner, your mother's impatient comments might have resulted from your inability to make a swift and clear decision about which dessert to have. If the comment also resonated at a deeper emotional level, perhaps that you were deeply conflicted about other choices in your life at the time, the lack of decisiveness about a dessert choice had a much deeper meaning than your mother could ever possibly have known. With each crossroads in life, you heard your mother's comment in the context of the present, loading layers and layers of meaning (and therefore emotion) upon a simple "hurry-up-and-choose-a-dessert" comment.

The memory of a painful experience has at least two components. One aspect of the pain memory contains the physical facts of the pain experience. The other component contains the emotions that accompany the memory. (Remember the IASP definition of pain: pain is an unpleasant sensory *and* emotional experience.) This phenomenon is easy to understand in the context of a phobia, such as fear of heights. The person may intellectually know that he/she is not going to fall out of the window, yet for all that supposed knowing, the experience of the emotion of fear overrules any cognitive overlay. If somehow the fear could be suspended, the brain could have a greater chance of rewriting the neural program. The problem arises when physical proximity to the window sends the phobic person into a non-rational and non-cognitive state where fear wins and cognition loses.

This idea of decoupling the emotion (fear) with the experience has led to some interesting new research endeavors exploring the role of the amygdala, a part of the brain that assigns meaning to an experience, especially with regard to fear. When neural input comes to the brain, it can take one of two possible paths, often called the high road or the low road.

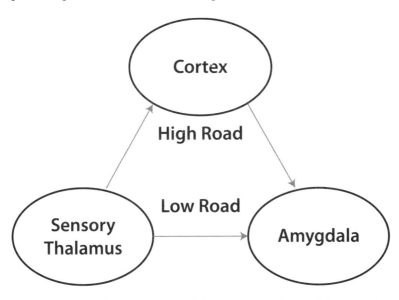

Figure 8.1: Joseph LeDoux's model of a low road and a high road for fear responses

When taking the low road, the neural pathway travels to the amygdala and then is shuffled immediately to the sensorimotor area of the brain, which then produces the physical experience of fear and/or pain. If the neural path takes the high road, the input goes upward from the amygdala to the cognitive area of the brain for more clarification. (The cognitive route was referred to as "top-down processing" in the last chapter.) The cognitive route is called the high road, because like taking a high trail on a hike, the high road takes longer and possibly consumes more energy.

There are times when the low road is absolutely appropriate in deciding if danger is lurking. Imagine that suddenly you see what seems to be a shadow coming towards your head. Should you stop and turn, looking in all directions to see what could account for the shadowy movement? That is not what your brain does, thankfully. It acts first (you duck), and you think later. The time it would take to cognitively review possible sources of danger would be far too long, and could make the difference between getting bonked on the head or not. The low road is extremely useful for survival but very dysfunctional when it becomes the *only* choice, like the war veteran who goes into a cold sweat every time he/she hears a loud noise. What was a useful response in the past (when the trauma was first experienced) is now no longer necessary or helpful. Short-term survival strategies are often terrible long-term patterns.

As I stated, the amygdala plays an important role in assigning meaning to these neural experiences. Research has demonstrated how important noradrenaline (the brain's adrenaline) is for the process of memory formation (University of Queensland 2008). Noradrenaline (also called norepinephrine) is produced in response to very powerful emotional events.

Many experiences of pain also have visual components, which present yet another significant obstacle to diffusing the power of a traumatic memory. Keith Payne and colleagues (Payne and Corrigan 2007) have shown that emotion and visual images have an effect that text alone cannot match. If you read a headline that says that a bomb exploded at a major city somewhere, it will not stay locked in your memory in the way that a picture of mutilated victims lying in the rubble will. Pictures, which become mental images, have a staying power. Emotion has been shown to make a memory much easier to retrieve than memories without any emotional content. Visual images often create very strong emotional responses, which then are harder to forget. I have had many clients with chronic back pain who were rather traumatized by the image of the X-ray of their back shown to them by a well-meaning physician. Having nondescript low back pain is one thing, but having a doctor show you this powerful image becomes a lasting, and often unhelpful, memory.

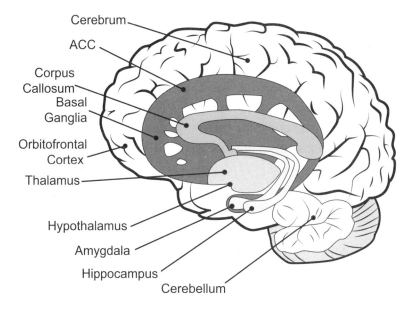

Figure 8.2: The location of various areas of the brain which may play a role in pain, including the amygdala and the hippocampus

There seems to be a very powerful inter-relationship involving the amygdala and the area of the brain called the hippocampus, where memory is stored. Researchers Dolcos, LaBar, and Cabeza (2005) explored the idea of a memory loop, where the memory (hippocampus) reinforces the emotion (amygdala), which then strengthens memory, etc. They showed subjects pictures of various scenes, some with emotional impact and others emotionally neutral. A year later, the subjects were again shown pictures, some of which were new and some of which they had seen a year earlier. While they were viewing these images, they were undergoing fMRI scans to observe brain activity. After one year, recall of emotionally powerful images was far better than for emotionally neutral pictures. While the subjects were correctly recalling the emotionally stronger pictures they had seen previously, the amygdala and the hippocampus both showed increased blood flow (more activity). The implication is that the emotion triggers recall, which, as the event is being remembered, triggers a stronger emotional reaction. This creates an endless loop of reinforcing the traumatic memory, which can play an important role in chronic pain.

This co-activation between the amygdala and the hippocampus is powerful, but it gets even more complicated because of the nature of the amygdala. Remember, the amygdala also receives sensory information. If that sensory information *feels* like fear, threat, or your typical response to pain, the amygdala is going to interpret the current sensory information as noxious.

As an example of misinterpretation of sensory data, if you were asked to describe the physical experience of excitement and anticipation of something wonderful about to happen, the physical experience will have much in common with what you would report if asked to describe the experience of fear. How do you know if what you are feeling is anticipation/excitement or anxiety/fear? Generally, the differentiation is determined from what you tell yourself about the meaning of the experience. The amygdala, however, can bypass the cognitive side of your brain and assign meaning to the sensory data before the "thinking you" gets to choose. Once the interpretation is determined, the amygdala may activate the hippocampus, looking for a memory that correlates to these physical and emotional experiences.

This is a remarkable directional shift from what has been assumed in psychology for many decades. In the old model, you experience an emotion, such as fear, and then your body reacts to that emotion by producing the physical attributes of fear such as restricted breathing, muscle tension, increased heart rate, etc. New research is revealing that when your body has the physical experience of fear, your brain looks through the archives for an emotion that matches your physical experience. Instead of the emotional producing the physical, the physical can produce the emotional.

In studying war veterans, the importance of the role of the amygdala in the experience of painful memories is confirmed by the fact that veterans who suffer damage to the amygdala do not seem capable of having PTSD (see the Recommended Reading section). Also, when researchers use shock to create fear conditioning in a rat, if a drug that dampens the amygdala is given to them, they have no memory that a certain conditioned event precedes a shock. Fear conditioning does not seem possible without contributions from the amygdala.

The use of pharmacological agents to influence traumatic memories has also been explored in humans. Brunet and Nader (Akerman 2006) have made some fascinating discoveries about PTSD. Based on work by Nader, Brunet experimented with giving PTSD patients the drug propranolol, which reduces activity in the amygdala. (Propranolol is commonly used to lower blood pressure. Roger Pitman and Larry Cahill were early researchers using this approach.) When patients under the influence of propranolol recalled the event that initiated the PTSD, they had greatly diminished amygdalar activity and therefore less fear. This allowed the patient to witness the event rather than experience it. Instead of being swept away by the physical experience of fear, the person was able to witness the experience as an observer.

When the emotions of the remembered event (mainly fear) steamroll the process, there is little possibility that the person will be able to dispassionately view the process from a cognitive perspective. Brunet's research with propranolol allowed the person to dispassionately observe his/her fear, showing us that any tool that can assuage fear gives a window of opportunity to re-evaluate the process from a more reasoned perspective.

Researchers are also using virtual reality exposure (VRE) to re-create and simulate combat situations in the treatment of PTSD (Rothbaum *et al.* 2001). This seems to have enormous potential, because researchers can control subtle details of the combat situation and slowly rewrite the neural response from the PTSD participant. The research is in its very early stages, but indeed looks very promising.

One other very new and very controversial aspect of drug therapy for painful memories is the use of a drug to block memory formation in the first place. When we are presented with new information, it is held in a fragile state before it is consolidated by the brain. It is the consolidation process you may have experienced when, after spending the evening taking your first ballroom dance lessons, you find yourself dancing in your dreams. Since memory is fragile up until the point it is consolidated, one possible strategy to prevent a negative memory from forming is to disrupt the consolidation process. An enzyme called PKMzeta has been identified as necessary for memory consolidation, and a substance called ZIP is its antagonist. Inject ZIP into the person and the memory never gets formed.

Blocking memory formation right after a traumatic event is highly controversial from an ethical standpoint. Drugs like propranolol dampen the amygdalar response to an already formed memory; drugs like ZIP actually stop the memory from forming in the first place. Even more controversially, these memory-blocking drugs aren't selective for just the bad stuff. It may take years to sort through the uses of this potential strategy in pain and memory.

Using the plasticity of memory to decrease pain

Questioning the accuracy of memory teaches us an important principle about the pain experience in general. When a person whose pain is from traumatic onset remembers the offending event repeatedly, how accurate is that memory? Is it possible that pain, especially chronic episodic pain, can be reconsolidated too? Each time we fear a relapse or experience a seemingly familiar pain, are we also rewriting the script and unconsciously altering details to make it worse? If we know that our memory of pain is suspect, can we observe the current experience of pain dispassionately (the high road), knowing that this strategy has been shown to decrease the experience of pain? There is great promise in learning to separate oneself from the fear that accompanies pain, distrusting our past memory of pain and learning to evaluate pain on present, rather than historical, terms.

Whether using virtual reality, hypnosis, or guidance by a therapist, being able to view the previously painful situation dispassionately is potentially a very powerful tool in rewriting our reaction to a previously painful circumstance. There is some new research into top-down cognitive influences currently being carried out. In one study (Depue, Curran, and Banich 2007), the researchers were able to teach people, through repeated exposures, not to respond to traumatic images using the pre-frontal part of the brain. There are parts of the brain that are activated in emotional suppression, the part of the brain that fires when your child accidentally spills milk for the umpteenth time and you know getting mad is not going to help the situation. Based on their research, Depue *et al.* suggest that this part of the brain (BA 10 and the superior, inferior, and middle FG for the brain scientists out there) can be used to control the emotional reactivity that accompanies the memory. This process takes quite a bit of repetition, but is promising data for people who suffer from fear of a painful past episode.

When fear leads to hyper-vigilance and catastrophizing

The brain has the marvelous ability to "round up" data, formulating a response with incomplete information. Rounding up is often called the brain's "best guess" scenario. This can be both an asset and a liability. As noted before, if you walk in the woods and you see something that resembles a snake, you don't stop to ponder whether it is or isn't a snake—you jump first and think later.

Here is another example. If you were sitting in a coffee shop and you noticed a friend pass by, what part of your brain should fire? Since you are seeing him or her, the region of your brain which houses the optic center (where vision is processed) should be activated. In reality, studies have shown that brain activity in the optic area is minimal; 80–90 percent of the activity occurs in the hippocampus, which is the area of the brain that processes memory. You do not really *see* your friend, you get enough data to clarify who it is, and then you fill in the rest of the details with memory. (No wonder I don't always recognize when my wife gets her hair cut—now at least I have some sort of neurobiological excuse. I am guessing this fact won't assuage my wife's disappointment!)

This is a life-saving mechanism of the brain, when used appropriately. However, when you are in the "best guess" mode your brain may apply the criteria far too broadly. The nervous system will then ramp up the fear program, seeing a harmless situation as a potential threat, especially if any part of it resembles a past experience of pain. Much like the hypersensitivity of the peripheral or central nervous system, hypersensitivity of fear mechanisms can exist; this phenomenon is called hyper-vigilance. Hyper-vigilance will skew the nervous system into perceiving threats when none exist. The cycle is self-perpetuating: the brain will misread innocuous data as a threat, thus confirming that a threat exists, which means heightening the sensory apparatus even further, which will then misinterpret more data and a vicious positive feedback loop is in place.

Constant fear which produces hyper-vigilance will typically create a related effect called catastrophizing, which means to perceive a stimulus in its most negative light or with its most negative outcome. One person with a stomach ache sees the discomfort as due to eating something disagreeable, while another person sees it as a possible ulcer in the making. If I have back discomfort, I could ascribe it to recent abnormal activity or misuse. For the person with a history of back pain, it is easy to perceive it as the harbinger of yet another interminably long bout with pain, just as it has been in the past. This perception (catastrophizing) sets up hyper-vigilance, which sets up peripheral sensitization, which leads to central sensitization, and soon the person is correct, they are truly suffering. This is perhaps why there is such a strong link between pain catastrophizing and pain disability.

Pain sufferers who tend to catastrophize often have decreased performance of their tasks of daily living, even tasks where cognition alone is demanded. It is quite interesting that evidence is beginning to show that people who catastrophize cannot avoid concentrating on the potentially devastating aspects of their pain. It may seem like a subtle point, but it doesn't seem that these people think about their pain all the time, they just cannot let go of it when other tasks are demanded of them.

One example of that effect is walking speed. If people have a history of back pain, they tend to be reticent to walk at a normal pace, not because it hurts, but because of fear that quick motion could be painful. The intriguing reality is that internal pressure on an intervertebral disc is actually less when you walk fast than during slow walking (McGill 2002). The back pain sufferer who slows the speed of walking to prevent pain unknowingly chooses a speed that actually increases the likelihood of pain. Sensing that walking, even slowly, produces pain, walking is slowly deleted from the list of safe activities for that back pain sufferer. Unfortunately, in reality, walking can be a great movement strategy/treatment for back pain when done correctly.

Fear of movement

Hyper-vigilance can be applied to many aspects of pain and one of the most common is movement. Let's examine fear of movement with regard to low back pain. Lower back pain (LBP) is the fifth most common reason people seek medical attention and the most common cause of movement limitation in the 45-year-old and younger set of the population (Laine, Goldman, and Wilson 2008).

When back pain strikes, it is most likely connected to movement. The sufferer notices that certain actions create pain while other movements or positions are relatively pain-free. Not surprisingly, the person will fear and thus avoid movements that create pain and instead seek positions of comfort. This fear of movement is called kinesiophobia; the process of restricting movement habits is called fear-avoidance theory.

In a short-term strategy (during acute pain), avoiding movements that create pain is quite useful. The problem ensues when a short-term strategy is "rounded up" by the brain and used long term. Like so many other aspects of pain, the short-term protective strategies that serve us well become counter-productive when applied in the long term.

When you want to move, your brain considers the intended outcome and then figures out a way to accomplish the action. Knowing what the final goal of the movement is, the brain recruits every muscle and neural pathway available to accomplish the intended action in the most efficient manner. Every simple action, such as bending over to tie your shoes, requires a symphony of muscular action to take place. No single muscle is involved; multiple muscles must turn on and off at precise times to accomplish even the most basic actions.

With such complexity, any disruption in the system can have vast consequences. When one muscle does not participate appropriately due to pain, or the memory of pain, other muscles must compensate by doing more. Over time, these overworked muscles may lose their sense of humor regarding their new job description.

Changing the recruitment pattern of muscles is analogous to driving down a road and then finding that a fallen tree has blocked the route. You still need to get where you are going, so an alternative route is employed. Unfortunately, as we know all too well, these alternative routes aren't often very efficient. What current research into muscle function is showing is that when the detour is removed (original pain), the brain still employs the inefficient detour. There is a redistribution of activity both within the muscle itself and also in the complex relationships between muscle groups. This limitation of movement alters normal muscle function which then can potentially lead to more pain in the future.

Dr. Paul Hodges has done some wonderful work with this subject (Hodges and Tucker 2011). His work has shown how pervasive these alterations are throughout the entirety of the muscular and nervous systems. By changing these muscle functions, we become less flexible in the broadest sense of the word. Our movement possibilities are limited, we become less efficient, and less adaptable in our nervous systems.

Who is most at risk for fear of movement? Surprisingly, research has shown that men are more likely than women to fear movement after a bout of pain. And, when age is taken into account, younger people are more affected than are older people. Surprising, isn't it?

Low back pain and bed rest

I would bet that many of you are old enough to remember when the medical community used to suggest that bed rest is an effective strategy for back pain. The idea was that if it hurts to move, then don't move: allow the body to heal. There was a time a few decades ago when this was common knowledge, a typical approach to back pain treatment. In fact, at one point, there was a rather heated debate whether two days of rest or one full week is better. This needed to be investigated. This debate began after a study concluded that two days of rest is better than one full week of bed rest (Deyo, Diehl, and Rosenthal 1986). When reassessing at three weeks and three months, the group that had just two days of rest were 45 percent better (measured by fewer days missed at work) than the seven-day group.

After this study was published, physicians were encouraged to recommend no more than two days of bed rest for the treatment of low back pain. The question of whether to advise bed rest at all was revisited in 1995.

To study the effectiveness of bed rest and back pain, three conditions were examined. One group was given with two days of rest, one group was given specific back exercises, and one group (the control group) who was told to continue their daily activities as much as possible.

The results of this study were surprising to all concerned. The low back pain sufferers assigned to a continuation of fairly normal activities (the control group) did much better than people assigned to bed rest or back exercises (Malmivaara *et al.* 1995). Exactly why continuing activity is more effective is not completely known, but it is reasonable that counteracting fear of movement is a possible explanation.

Related to fear and movement is the phenomenon of freezing and pain, something that has received a fair amount of attention in the scientific community lately. Freezing is well known in animal experiments in fear and is currently being explored in humans also. Fear produces an activation of the sympathetic nervous system, which then creates a predictable set of actions in the nervous system, all meant for survival. Blood pressure increases, blood is diverted from non-essential tasks (survivally speaking) like digestion and reproduction to the muscles of the extremities to be used for fighting or fleeing. This is called the fight or flight mechanism, well publicized in the stress research literature. Less known outside the scientific community is the "freeze mode," which happens before fight or flight. In some cases, freezing is a protective strategy in itself; fighting or fleeing is not always the best option for survival.

Beyond the obvious example of an opossum, this is seen in the animal world quite frequently. When a lion chases down a gazelle, sometimes the gazelle will collapse into a seemingly lifeless (freeze) state at the first touch of the lion's paw upon its flank. There are times when the lion is doing the chase for fun and training, and a prey that provides no resistance is no fun at all. Satisfied that his/her abilities as a hunter are sharp, the lion walks away. When the lion is no longer around, the gazelle will come back to "life." How it awakens is very interesting and can be observed in other animals in the wild. After the freeze mode, the instinctive response is to awaken by shaking rather violently, a sort of primal shivering. Once this shivering/shaking process is completed, the animal walks away.

What one cannot help but wonder is whether this primal post-freeze movement is a method of release that prevents the pain and fear from being "stuck" in the neural circuitry. Clinicians in the psychological field have been exploring this phenomenon in humans (Levine 1997; Ogden, Minton, and Pain 2006; Scaer 2001). It is leading to new understanding about pain, fear, and the freeze process.

There are times when the freeze process is shortened, such as during the seconds just before movement is seen as the choice for survival. This brief freeze process is called the orienting response, a phase that lasts for about four seconds or so. It has been said that the brain asks three questions of every stimulus: what is it? What does it mean? What do I do? The orienting response refers to a pause while the brain gathers the relevant information to make these decisions. If an unexpected noise happens somewhere in your immediate vicinity, your first reaction (after the reflexive jump) is to freeze in order to assess what just happened, where it came from, and how you should respond. This is like a mini-freeze, one done as a temporary strategy, just before embarking on a course of action.

After a freeze, movement should then occur, either into (fight) or away from (flight) the potential threat. Applied to low back pain sufferers, the initial inhibition of movement functions much like a freeze state, a strategy that makes perfect sense. During back pain, it is common that painful movements are very directionally specific, that is, it hurts if I bend forward but not if I bend backward. In the initial stages of pain, one would need to know exactly which movements are problematic and thus avoid further irritation. Instead of limiting movement to only these specific offending actions, we quite often choose, consciously or unconsciously, to limit all back movement. This restriction of motion slowly becomes a pattern which will likely create unnoticed limitations and ultimately perpetuate the pain. Some back pain experts, most notably Dr. John Sarno, encourage people to move and overcome the fear of pain. Eschewing any mechanical reasons for back pain, Sarno's main treatment is cognitive, encouraging and empowering the sufferer to resume a normal active life. While his methodology is unconventional and has ruffled a lot of feathers in the orthopedic world, the results of his strategies are quite impressive.

Fear of movement has another very interesting aspect, one that Patrick Wall, perhaps the most highly regarded pain researcher, hypothesized about before his death. When pain is experienced, different areas of the brain tend to light up, as seen through fMRI scans. Surprisingly, or perhaps not if you think about it, the pre-motor area of the brain also lights up. The pre-motor area of the brain is the area that controls volitional movement. Before I raise my finger to scratch my nose, the pre-motor area part of my brain will fire, which precedes the actual movement of my finger upward.

With pain, the pre-motor area lights up (is activated) when pain is experienced. Wall hypothesized that movement is a way for pain to consummate, meaning to finish or complete itself. His idea was that movement is essential to pain relief and that any approach to pain reduction should ultimately involve movement. As I write these particular words, I happen to be on a flight from San Francisco to Chicago. As you probably have experienced, the restriction of movement resulting from coach seating in an airplane these days can be a pain in the butt in the most literal sense.

The natural response to pain is the desire to move. That movement can take the form of a shifting of positions or a massive and explosive dash away from the danger. Wall suggested that restricting movement is a way of somehow locking the neural circuit that houses the pain mechanism in a holding pattern, perhaps ultimately leading to chronic pain. This is a very interesting idea and requires further exploration.

Movement inhibits pain

There is another reason why movement is an antidote to pain, one that is again tied to a protective function in the brain. This mechanism called descending inhibition. Descending inhibition is your brain's ability to dampen pain when you are fully engaged in an essential activity. For instance, if an attacker was chasing you and threw a knife into your leg, you would be astonished at how fast you can run with a knife sticking out of your pants! In all likelihood, you would not have noticed the knife and subsequent wound until you were safe. How is it possible that a knife wound to your leg is not painful?

The answer is the descending inhibition system, which protects you by dampening pain until you are safely out of reach. This is a very important evolutionary protective mechanism. Pain is not helpful or protective if you are running for your life. As a result, your brain blunts the pain experience until you are once again safe. Parents have also seen this effect in children who return home after aggressively playing outside, only to discover there is some dried blood on a pants leg of the child. Upon discovering (seeing) the blood, the child now erupts in tears.

The protective effect of descending inhibition can then be used as another potential tool to combat pain. When you are active, your brain assumes that this movement is necessary for survival and will, after a short period of time, start decreasing pain to allow you to move more comfortably. It is a common experience for many that when one begins to exercise, the first segment in time is not exactly comfortable, but improves with increased activity. When I get on my bike and start pedaling, I have about 30 excuses per mile as to why today isn't a good day to ride. After a few miles, I start to feel better and the pedaling is easier: descending inhibition in action. In the initiation of activity, the brain says, "Are you sure you want to do this?" If you persist, the nervous system will make movement easier, thinking that, because you persist, the action must be necessary.

This is also a reasonable explanation as to why exercise can be so important for both pain and stress reduction. As we have seen, pain lights up the pre-motor area of the brain. Stress sends blood to the periphery in anticipation of possible flight or confrontation. Movement or exercise is a way to translate that preparation into action. Again, in experiments with rats, stress levels in response to electric shock went down if the rat had something to chew on to release his/her frustration. (If no wood was available, the rat would chew on another rat!) Movement is an important key to releasing the frustration of stress and pain. (For more information about stress, read the research and writing of Robert Sapolsky 2004.)

Diagnosis and fear

A while ago, I heard an interview with a prominent magazine editor, and the interviewer happened to ask him about his personal health issues. This editor had experienced some very strange neural symptoms, which his local physicians diagnosed as Lyme disease. After two years without improvement, he went to Mayo Clinic for a full work-up. First, Mayo did a very thorough work-up and found that he was originally misdiagnosed; he did not, in fact, have Lyme disease. Second, the doctors and the editor compiled a list of every possible malady that could possibly be associated with his symptoms. In essence, the doctors asked this man what diseases he was worried about, and if it was reasonable, they tested for it.

In the end, he left the clinic with no specific diagnosis and was taken off all the useless medicine he was ingesting for a condition he did not have. The doctors also pointed out that whatever this malady was, it had not been getting worse over the last 16 months, so it was highly unlikely that this unknown problem was a progressive neural disease. Imagine what this information did for this man's fear with regard to his pain; essentially every disease that he was worried about was removed from the list. Moreover, and amazingly, the doctors did not feel the need to give his condition a name.

Imaging as reality

In the age of perceiving diagnostic imaging as absolute truth, we have drifted away from good medicine. Instead of valuing the doctor's clinical judgment, the insurance companies need to see something on an MRI or X-ray scan to validate a diagnosis. Unfortunately, in many cases, the image is not only unhelpful, it can also be misleading. For example, if a patient has back pain and is required to have an X-ray taken, the odds are quite high that there will be a fair amount of arthritis in the lumbar spine. Having the arthritis pointed out in the X-ray, the patient often feels like there is no recourse except acceptance of a lifelong sentence of pain.

The facts are, however, that if you X-ray 60 people who are age 55 and older, it would be startling *not* to see arthritic changes in the spine. Moreover, if you took those 60 X-rays and bet a radiologist (for $10,000, just to up the ante) that she/he couldn't pick the two people in the most pain, it is doubtful that a radiologist would accept the wager. The radiologists often know better, but patients and the insurance companies want a visible reason for the pain. The arthritic diagnosis is convenient, but often very misleading. I have had clients confess that they severely curtailed their activities after getting the arthritis diagnosis, which is exactly the wrong strategy, given the current research.

Even more damning, Chou *et al.* (2009) found that people who were given an MRI didn't have any better outcomes than those who were treated without one. In fact, people who did get an MRI *did worse* overall! That created a bit of a firestorm in the medical community. For all the added expense of the MRI imaging, these people did worse. How in the world can that be?

There are two reasonable explanations for this outcome. One of them was eloquently stated by the study author Dr. Roger Chou:

> You can find lots of stuff on X-rays and M.R.I.'s like degenerative disks and arthritis, but these things are very weakly correlated with low back pain. We think we're helping patients by doing a test, but we're adding cost, exposing people to radiation and people may be getting unnecessary surgery. They start to think of themselves as having a horrible back problem and they stop doing exercise and things that are good for them, when in reality, a lot of people have degenerative disks and arthritis and have no pain at all. (Chou *et al.* 2009)

After reading the chapter in this book on pain and meaning, you can see that Dr. Chou's insightful comments are right on target. Imagine a patient coming home after meeting with his physician, getting the diagnosis of a disc herniation, and seeing the protruding disc on his MRI. After relaying the news to his wife, she then asks if he would like to join her and the family dog for their evening walk. Can't you just see him balking now, worrying that perhaps he should limit his activity because he has a serious problem with his back? This is exactly the wrong strategy; the more sedentary he becomes the worse his back is going to be, which then confirms his idea that something is really wrong with his back. Worse yet, he could *see* it.

Second, if a healthcare provider sees something unusual on the screen, the temptation is to treat what is found. Unfortunately, the treatment process itself can be a source of further pain and suffering; something that I am sure you have experienced or witnessed in others. Negative effects from treatment are even harder to accept given the distinct possibility that what was treated may have nothing to do with the original pain.

A wonderful example of diagnostic imaging being potentially deceptive is the realm of disc problems and low back pain. After the publication of a famous paper by Mixter and Barr (1934), the understanding that disc prolapse could cause sciatic pains ushered in what is commonly called the "Dynasty of the Disc." After the advent of MRI, the diagnostic world was even more excited since the intrusion of the disc onto the spinal cord was now visible on the image. This validated Mixter and Barr's ideas, and disc issues were widely seen as the source of much, if not most, of back pain.

While this all seems positive and an advancement, think about who gets a lumbar spine MRI. MRIs are very expensive, so only patients with back pain get them. While this seems obvious, what about people who never have back pain? What do their spinal discs look like? A study by Jensen *et al.* (1994) examined just that question: 98 people who had never had any back pain were given MRIs, which showed serious disc issues in 64 percent of the group! Other researchers have made similar findings. Because we see pathology on the image, the temptation is to assume that the pathology we see is present only in the person with the malady. Unfortunately, we don't really know what "normal" is.

I treated a client recently who had back discomfort with pain also radiating down his leg. This client was the consummate academician and wanted to deeply understand his problem. I could tell that he wasn't exactly thrilled about seeing a Precision Neuromuscular Therapist; he was looking for a treatment approach that, in his mind, was more science based. (In fact, when I asked him why he came to see me, he replied that his wife made him!) After describing his symptoms, he explained his fears about his condition and what it might mean for his teaching and research workload. After explaining some basic physiology, he and I did an overview of the literature together. After my giving him a research direction, he explored the subject thoroughly, exposing me to studies I had never seen, for which I was very grateful; some of them are part of this book! One of his major fears was something that a surgeon alluded to: that not doing surgery was risky and could lead to disastrous and irreversible consequences.

This fear of irreversible consequences was addressed in a study by Weinstein *et al.* (2006). Over 2000 sciatic pain patients were divided into two groups, one having back surgery and the other not. In the end, the outcomes for both groups were about the same. Quite a few doctors refused to put their patients into the non-surgical group, saying that it was unethical to deny them surgery, knowing that severe and irreversible damage could result. In the end, not one person in the study had anything like that happen. The fear (for both patient and doctor) that accompanies a non-surgical approach now seems unfounded.

On a different note, a study by Masui *et al.* (2005) followed people who had disc abnormalities for a period of seven years. While all of the subjects continued to present with increased degenerative changes (according to the MRI, done at two years and then again seven years later), there was no correlation between the degeneration and the patient's report of pain. Meaning, if you looked at the MRIs at the seven-year mark, you could not tell who was in pain and who wasn't. This has been shown in several other studies. Looking at the presence of a disc problem on an MRI doesn't tell you much about whether what you see on the screen is responsible for the pain the person is experiencing. Unfortunately, you cannot see pain on a screen; what we see is something that we *believe* to be correlated with pain.

When the academician arrived for his next appointment with me, his physical presentation was entirely different. Gone was the man who seemed so powerless; he was replaced by someone who felt he had some control over his destiny. I don't know if his back actually hurt less (I doubt that it did), I think he just didn't notice it as much and he was no longer worried about it. He clearly seemed to relish having more control over where this process was going, a desirable goal for many people in pain.

My academician client decided to share the research with his primary care doctor, a very good physician who was a willing partner in this whole process. Other than as a source of information, I played almost no role in his recovery, as my client did not feel my soft-tissue work helped him as much as walking and being active. His doctor and I were both observers and advisors. In the end, he did magnificently and has had no recurrence of his back pain. The real healing came in the form of knowledge, which was the antidote to his fear.

What do we take away from this? First, we have to resist seeing this in black and white terms. This *does not* mean that MRIs are useless and should not be given to patients. It certainly does, however, create a challenge for the healthcare system. This will take a shift of thinking on all sides of the issue. Patients need to stop pressuring doctors to use every available technology to create a diagnosis. On the other hand, if the doctor doesn't do that, they can be sued. Perhaps, someday, we can let doctors be doctors and not practice defensive medicine. Doctors must, however, use sound clinical judgment based on evidence. Having a physician who is a partner in the process of decision-making is of utmost importance. One of the substantial benefits of the partnership approach to the doctor–patient relationship is the sense of control it gives the patient, and that sense of control lessens the experience of pain.

Fear and sense of control

One example of this application of patient control is the advent of Patient Controlled Analgesia (PCA) in hospital settings. PCA is very popular with patients, especially those in areas of the hospital with lower nurse-to-patient ratios.

The image is an easy one to conjure, one that many hospital patients have experienced over the years. After a surgical event, the patient is put into a hospital room where the nursing staff is now administering care. At some point, the nurse comes in to see how you are doing. (This is usually just at the point when sleep has begun.) Feeling better than you expected, you decline the use of further pain medication. Later, however, you rethink that decision and decide that the pain might be increasing, or you are worried that it might intensify. You ring for the nurse. Time continues and the pain seems to be getting worse. Another staff person comes into the room, but this person cannot administer meds. She says the nurse is really busy, but will be right there as soon as he/she can. Meanwhile, you fear that your pain will get out of control. When the nurse finally comes, you thankfully accept the pain medication. Next time, you will take the meds even though you do not feel you need them, just to prevent being in a situation where you are dependent on the nurse to come and administer them.

PCA is a radical departure from this scenario. With the medication connected to an IV unit, the patient can self-administer medication at will. In the old paradigm, healthcare providers were nervous that patients would help themselves to copious amounts of pain medication, inviting a host of other problems, most notably dependence. In reality, the opposite has proven to be true (plus there are controls on the machine—it has a lock-out mechanism to prevent administering too much in a defined time). PCA has resulted in a small *decrease* in the amount of medication consumed by the patient. When people know they will have the medication needed at the time of their choosing, the fear of scarcity is diminished. In reality, the clinical numbers don't show PCA to be significantly more effective than meds administered by the nurse, but the patient satisfaction is far greater for PCA than for conventional methods. The numbers may not be better, but the patient *feels* better about the process. As this fear diminishes, the experience of pain also lessens.

It is likely that a good part of the patient satisfaction with PCA is the sense of control over the situation. Some of the evidence from clever experiments by Jay Weiss shows that the control doesn't even have to work (Sapolsky 2004)! Give a rat a series of electric shocks and then train it to press a lever to stop the shocks from happening. The rat now knows how to control the pain: it just presses the lever. Now, repeat the experiment but take the lever away and the rat is under severe stress. You have removed the one strategy the rat knows can make the pain stop. Here is what is wild; reintroduce the lever into the experiment, except this time the lever doesn't work, and the stress levels in the rat still decrease. The rat's stress response lowers simply by the act of doing something it believes will work, even though it isn't working now. Like the rat, we feel better when we are actually doing something about the pain, rather than helplessly suffering through it.

Another example of sense of control and resulting stress levels was revealed in research by Bourne (Bourne, Rose, and Mason 1968) on soldiers in Vietnam. He looked at the cortisol (a measure of stress) levels of soldiers on the day before an

133

expected Viet Cong attack and the day afterward. The study compared groups of soldiers with different tasks: radio operators and regular combat soldiers. Strangely, the cortisol levels of the combat soldiers dropped on the day before an expected attack, while the cortisol levels of the radio operators went up substantially. The explanation that Bourne put forth was that the combat soldiers had a day of intense regimented activity in preparation for the attack; perhaps they were too busy to think about what was to come. In contrast, the radio operators knew about the impending attack before anyone else but could do nothing to prepare; they were forced to sit and wait. The radio operators had knowledge, but no control.

If fear can produce an increase in the experience of pain, is no fear at all a desirable goal? Surprisingly, the answer seems to be no. In an interesting study of patients who were going to undergo abdominal surgery, people who went into the operation with no seeming concern at all did not do well after surgery (Lawndy *et al.* 2011; Sime 1976). They were often anxious and displayed anger and resentment towards the staff of the hospital. On the other hand, those people who had very high levels of fear before the operation also struggled after the surgery. The group that displayed the best post-surgery outcomes had reasonable fear which prompted them to ask relevant questions to the staff about what to expect. In this case, fear prompted the patient to ask questions, which decreases unpredictability, which lowers pain levels.

In summary, fear is an important part of the mystery of pain because it can intensify the feelings of pain, cause the person to avoid movement and activity, and be part of a conditioned response that sets up further pain. As with the theme of this book, a deeper understanding of the process is a powerful tool in negating the effects of fear and anxiety in the pain experience. Lessening fear and restoring a sense of control is an important step to decreasing pain and restoring function.

CHAPTER 9

PLACEBOS AND THE PLACEBO EFFECT

I believe, therefore I heal

One of the most fascinating and often controversial aspects of pain research is the placebo effect, which has received much attention over the last few years. Before we go further, we should define *placebo* and the *placebo effect*. A placebo is an inert substance or treatment that produces no known effect on a symptom, disease, or condition. The placebo effect refers to the change in a person's condition from the administration of this innocuous or inert substance or action. In other words, a placebo has no known value, but it produces an effect on the body as though it did have healing properties. The word placebo originates from the Latin *placer* which means "to please." The placebo effect is generally thought to be short-lived, whereas a long-term benefit from an inert substance or treatment might be termed a "confidence cure."

In pain research, the placebo effect refers to the phenomenon that pain will decrease with the power of belief in the intervention. If a person believes that a powerful drug has been administered, he/she will experience the effects of the drug, even if what was administered was merely a sugar pill. Even more remarkable, the subject may also experience any side-effects of the drug he/she believes to be receiving and may also go through withdrawal symptoms when the placebo is no longer administered. This has astounding implications for all of healthcare and confirms the power of belief to make us well or make us sick. This subject is controversial and fraught with potential downsides, yet placebos can have an upside potential that is worthy of deeper exploration.

One of the early proponents of the placebo effect was a physician named Henry K. Beecher, a field-hospital clinical pharmacologist in Italy and North Africa in World War Two. Dr. Beecher noticed that some soldiers who were seriously injured needed very little pain medication while others with lesser wounds needed much more. Dr. Beecher questioned the reason for the difference, theorizing that for some soldiers being in the hospital meant safety and recovery. The observation that the experience of pain could be changed by the soldier's thoughts and emotions spurred Dr. Beecher to clarify that pain is not just a physical stimulus but is an emotional experience as well. His exploration of the power of belief, expectation, and the role of emotions helped to open a new avenue in pain research.

In addition, his ideas about the placebo effect changed the way pharmacological research is done, adding in controlled double blind studies to negate the power of the patient's belief in the drug given. If the patient has significant improvement from the drug he/she is taking and that drug (unknowingly to the recipient) is really an inert substance like a sugar pill, then belief and expectation are likely responsible for the improvement. A viable drug or alternative approach must surpass the placebo effect, which typically can be in the range of 35 percent. Some of the effectiveness rates for placebos in different conditions are astounding: one meta-analysis of placebo studies of antidepressants concluded that the placebos had an effectiveness rate of 79 percent.

One possible explanation for the effectiveness of placebos is the manifestation of the power of belief; another explanation is the power of conditioning in our nervous systems. Let's begin with the power of belief and expectation first.

In the chapter on "Attention and Pain," I referred to an excellent study of the power of expectation by Sawamoto and colleagues, exploring the expectation of pain with the application of hot or warm stimulus to the arm. Using fMRI, the researchers examined the brain activity of subjects who were told that a hot device would be placed on the forearm. When the hot stimulus was applied, areas of the brain that were associated with pain lit up. When the subjects were told a warm stimulus would be applied to the arm instead, the activation in those same regions of the brain was markedly subdued. When the subjects were told that a hot application was going to be applied, but actually a warm stimulus was applied instead, the brain activity was identical to the painful (hot) stimulus. In other words, the subjects expected pain and responded to warmth as though it were exceedingly hot and painful. Expectation clearly influences perception of reality.

Sawamoto's study explores the opposite of the placebo effect, the *nocebo* effect. Instead of the belief that something has healing powers, the nocebo effect refers to the belief that something is harmful when it really is not. This can be just as powerful as a placebo, but in the other direction.

A twist on the nocebo effect is this: it is not uncommon for people who improved in a placebo study to suddenly worsen when they discover that the successful intervention was a sham. The positive placebo effect was quickly erased by the knowledge that the intervention was not "real." It is quite striking when you think about it: positive belief makes the person better but non-belief erases many of the tangible gains. Perhaps instead of focusing completely on the power of "things" (medications and treatments), we should be equally awed by the inherent power of our mind to affect health at every level.

Not surprisingly, and perhaps unfortunately, there is a clear relationship between the cost of an intervention and its perceived effectiveness. Dan Ariely has done several extremely clever (and somewhat disconcerting) studies to explore perceptions about cost. In one study done by Ariely's student Rebecca Waber (Waber *et al.* 2008), subjects were asked to test the effectiveness of a new drug (which was actually a placebo) from China called "Veladone-RX." Subjects were given electric shocks to measure pain tolerance and then given the drug to test its pain-relieving qualities. One group was told that this new drug was obtained at a substantial discount (about 10 cents vs. a normal cost of $2.50 per pill). The other group was shown the brochure for the medicine and was told it was $2.50 per dose (full cost). The group that understood that the medicine (which was really a sugar pill) was inexpensive got less benefit than the group who thought the medicine was $2.50 per pill. Think of the implications. If the intervention, whatever it is, is expensive, we think it is more effective. We seem to equate cost with effectiveness.

Dr. Ariely has also done similar experiments with energy drinks. Subjects were given a sham energy drink with slick marketing brochures. The subjects in the study were to exercise strenuously and then rate the effectiveness of the drink in combating resulting fatigue. Subjects who got the discounted energy drink (89¢ vs. the full price of $2.89) got less benefit from the drink. Those who thought the drink was $2.89 got the most benefit (Shiv, Carmon, and Ariely 2005).

While the cost is an obvious factor in the effectiveness, so is the placebo effect as a whole. Remember, the subjects who were given a discounted pill or a full price pill were both unknowingly getting a sugar pill. The effectiveness rate of the discount pill was still a whopping 61 percent. (The full price group had an effectiveness rate of 85%.) Those are astounding success rates no matter what the intervention. Such is the power of the mind.

In placebo drug studies, there are certain truths. Two pills are better than one. A larger pill is better than a smaller pill. Injections are better than pills. The more severe the pain, the more effective a placebo is. It would be tempting to think that the placebo effect is applicable to the taking of medications, but not much else. That would be a very incorrect assumption. The taking of a sugar pill is one thing, but placebo surgery is another. Yes, even placebo surgery has been studied and the results are astounding.

In a landmark study (Moseley *et al.* 2002), researchers wanted to study the effectiveness of arthroscopic surgery of the knee. This is an increasingly popular operation, with over 650,000 done annually at the time of the study. The average cost of the procedure is about $5000. What these researchers wanted to know, as does any practitioner or provider, is what the effect of the intervention is and whether it alters the normal course of events (doing nothing).

In this case, 180 cases were examined and told that they would have either regular arthroscopic knee surgery, a washing of the joint with saline (called lavage), or possibly a sham surgery. Each group was prepped and taken in for surgery in normal fashion. In arthroscopic surgery of the knee and lavage, three small wounds are made around the knee for lubricating the joint, observation, and removal of debris. In the placebo cases, the wounds were made, but no entrance into the tissue was done. In the other cases, a standard arthroscopic (group 2) or lavage procedure (group 3) was done. Patients would not be able to tell the difference (whether they had the debridement, lavage, or sham procedure) as the entrance wounds would look the same.

All patients were observed for two years after the surgery. Follow-up assessments are typically done at multiple points to discern effectiveness over time. Most remarkably, at one point the placebo group was faring better than the other two groups who had the "real" procedure. In the end, the outcomes for all three groups were about the same.

As you can imagine, this study created a firestorm of ethical backlash for deceiving people into thinking that they had had surgery when they did not. Getting beyond the ethical discussion, the subjects in the study who underwent the placebo surgery did as well as those who got the real procedure. This same placebo approach has been used to study both Parkinson's disease and psoriasis. Cynthia McRae and colleagues (McRae *et al.* 2004) reported that patients with advanced Parkinson's, who believed that they had received an implantation of embryonic dopamine cells into the brain, did as well as patients who actually received the true implantation. These are serious conditions and placebos seem to be serious medicine.

In these placebo studies performed on humans, the subjects believed that the substance or therapeutic intervention has some sort of healing power. However, the placebo effect also works on animals, which points to conditioning as another possible explanation for the positive effect of a placebo. For example, consider the research of Maj-Britt Niemi (Pacheco-Lopez *et al.* 2009). In this research, immune suppressant drugs that are often given in preparation for organ transplants were administered to mice. At the same time as the immunosuppressant drugs (cyclosporine A) were given, the researchers gave mice sweetened water. After multiple experiences combining the drug administration and sweetened water, the mice became conditioned to lower their immune systems whenever they drank the sweetened water (markers that show immune function had decreased at essentially the same rate as if they had taken the drug cyclosporine A). Here is a case of pure conditioning, rather than a belief-driven (expectations-driven) system. (It is doubtful that the mice had a belief about the effects of the sweetened water!)

As a basis for the power of conditioning being a possible explanation of placebo effectiveness, we return to the pioneering work of Ivan Pavlov, who won the Nobel Prize for medicine in 1904. Pavlov explored the power of the mind to learn and relearn;

much like rewriting the "software" that runs our responses to the environment around us. In his famous experiments, he was able to condition dogs to respond to stimuli, like the famous salivation experiments where upon hearing a bell enough times as a dog was being fed, the sound of the bell alone would make the dog salivate. Apply conditioning now to another situation, such as getting an infusion of an intravenous anesthetic to quieten pain so a patient can rest well. If the anesthetic has been used multiple times with success, the patient will derive the same result (pain decrease and resulting sleep) from an intravenous drip of weak saline solution. This is a conditioned response and the saline solution is a placebo. Did you ever wonder why the intravenous drip bags are held within a perfect line of sight of the patient? Yes, part of that is for the nurse, so that she/he can see it. Perhaps more importantly, it is for the benefit of the patient. Being told that the pain medications are being administered is one thing, seeing them dripping into the bag is something else.

This conditioning effect is also demonstrated by research from Marion U. Goebel (Goebel *et al.* 2008). She gave an allergy medication coupled with an unusual drink to 30 people who suffered from allergies to dust mites. After several successful doses of the real medication coupled with the unusual drink, she then substituted a placebo that looked exactly like the real drug. The patients who received the placebo coupled with the unusual drink had the same reduction in allergic reactions as though they had taken the real drug. Those who got the placebo drug with water instead of the unusual drink got no results. The brain had linked the unusual drink and the medication together, just as the mice had done with the immunosuppressant medication and the sweetened water. Our brain has a tendency to bind experiences together, for good or for ill.

Two parts of the brain that seem active in the placebo phenomena are the amygdala and the hippocampus, both parts of the brain that keep resurfacing in our exploration of the mystery of pain. The amygdala processes information related to the emotional content of a stimulus while the hippocampus is the memory center of the brain. The amygdala seems to be the active component of the expectation/belief aspect of placebos, while the hippocampus seems to be the center which is involved in their conditioned response effect.

Promising work in the field of fMRI reveals that placebo effectiveness may also be tied to activating a part of the brain called the nucleus accumbens (NAcc). The nucleus accumbens is rather like the pleasure and reward center of the brain, an area that is often studied in addiction, gambling, food, and sex. When the NAcc lights up, the dopamine floods the area and extreme pleasure is the result. In the 1950s, research by Olds and Milner brought the NAcc to light (Olds and Milner 1954). Rats with an electrode planted in the NAcc would rather keep stimulating that part of their brain (they had the power to do that by pushing a lever which sent a stimulus to the NAcc) than eat or drink. This research shed light on drug addiction to substances like cocaine. As it turns out, a somewhat similar process happens with a placebo. The pleasure center also lights up with the *expectation* of reward, not just the reward itself. Harkening back to the addiction studies, you might have read studies where people (especially adolescents) got very drunk (because they expected to) on what they found out later wasn't an alcoholic drink at all. This, of course, was quite embarrassing to the young people who were fooled into thinking they were drinking very strong liquor.

Is belief necessary for a placebo to be effective?

Interestingly, it has always been thought that for placebos to be effective, the receiver (patient) must not know it is a placebo and they must believe that the substance or intervention has the power to heal. Unfortunately for healthcare providers, this can lead to an ethical dilemma. If you have to deceive your patient, it can erode patient trust if the use of a placebo intervention is later revealed. If the patient believes the medicine is real, then deception is part of the treatment, a fact that makes many providers understandably uncomfortable. As it turns out, this may not be necessary.

Dr. Ted Kaptchuk, along with a team of researchers, looked at whether knowing the substance was a placebo would diminish the benefits (Kaptchuk *et al.* 2010). In a clever study, they gave medicines to 80 patients who suffered from Irritable Bowel Syndrome, who were then split into two groups. The patients who received a placebo were aware that the "drug" they were receiving was a placebo. The medicine was clearly marked as a placebo and the patient was informed that "placebo pills, something like sugar pills, have been shown in rigorous clinical testing to produce significant mind–body self-healing processes." Remarkably, patients who knew they were getting placebos *still* had a significant improvement. This may mean that deception is not a necessary part of the process. As these patients were informed that placebos have been shown to be effective, perhaps belief and expectation are still essential elements. Still, the fact that an inert substance can be effective even if patients are aware they are taking a placebo is nothing short of remarkable. When we hear the term placebo, we often equate this with something of no value, a sham treatment akin to deception or snake oil. While that *may* be true, the placebo effect represents the power of the mind to create real physical effects. This is not something to be looked down upon. It is perhaps important to understand the difference between the placebo effect in a drug trial and the placebo effect in the doctor's office.

In research, the placebo effect is something to be controlled and eliminated, if possible. It muddies the water of true science and confounds research outcomes. While researchers want to know if a particular intervention has merit, the actual context in which the therapy will be delivered is quite different from the lab in which it was researched. As any pragmatic primary physician will affirm (and I have found primary care physicians to be extremely pragmatic), if the goal is to create an effect, how it is attained is less important than getting the intended result. As many physicians have said to their patients, "If you feel that taking or doing XXX is helping you, by all means continue to do it. As long as there is no downside, and doing/taking something does not replace a proven approach, what is the harm?"

I would bet that many of you have had the caring reassurance of a compassionate healthcare provider calm you when your pain created much needless fear and anxiety simply because the cause of those symptoms was unknown. Conversely, I am sure many of you have suffered negative experiences with providers whose people-skills left much to be desired. Imagine an oncologist counseling a patient who has had a recurrence of her cancer. Imagine the power of the wording "if" the cancer returns vs. "when" the cancer returns. Yes, the odds are the cancer will return, but this is not a guarantee, just odds. The use of the term "when" could be devastating for the patient. No one truly knows whether it is "if" or "when," so why not give hope to the patient? If the delivery of an intervention can maximize results, we should embrace the placebo effect as another tool in our arsenal against suffering and pain.

The presentation by the provider as to the value of the intervention is extremely important to the success of the therapy. Research has shown that if the physician emphasizes the side-effects and low probabilities of a particular medicine, the effectiveness rate suffers. If the physician suggests that this particular drug is the hottest thing on the market and the success rate is terrific, it is not surprising that the effectiveness rate of the medicine is high.

This fact that belief is so important to outcome is a hard pill to swallow for many healthcare providers. It is one thing for an acupuncturist or alternative healthcare provider to be accused of providing nothing but a sham/placebo treatment for his/her patients. It is another for an orthopedist to be faced with the same charge. In truth, both can be true. The same can be said about every field of healthcare. In the end, the best approach seems to be to acknowledge the power of belief and to carefully use it for good. This necessitates a vigilant grasp on ethical behavior, making sure that any placebo effect is for the benefit of the patient and not the practitioner.

PHANTOM LIMB PAIN
You don't have to have a leg to have leg pain

A common theme of this book is that pain is not something easily detected using diagnostic imaging technology. Phantom limb pain exemplifies that principle in the extreme—it is the experience of pain in a limb that does not exist! How can one have the experience of pain in an arm that isn't there? If you are committed to the old model of pain as a beneficent warning of impending damage, the phenomenon of phantom limb pain just doesn't make any sense.

Phantom limb pain is pain that is felt in a limb that has been removed, such as a leg that was amputated after severe trauma. How common is phantom pain after amputation? The reported rate of phantom limb pain in amputees is about 80 percent. Conflicts like the wars in Iraq and Afghanistan are producing hundreds of soldiers who have lost limbs due to the devastating effects of improvised explosive devices (IEDs). These soldiers have suffered greatly from the initial injury, let alone having continued pain in the absent limb. Phantom pain can take many forms but is most commonly a burning or itching sensation, which is why it was so easy for doctors to assume phantom pain was the result of a nerve injury (burning and itching are common neural symptoms). Other common phantom limb sensations are the feeling that the absent limb is contracted, cold, or is held in a strange position. It is not uncommon for the phantom pain or discomfort to resemble what the person experienced before amputation. If the arm was held in a sling for months while waiting to see if recovery was possible, it is typical for the phantom arm to have the same curled presentation it had while being supported in the sling. People who have phantom limb pain also often have the sensation of telescoping, a feeling that the phantom is shrinking up inside the existing limb, the way an umbrella can be telescoped from the extended position to a compressed state. This is present in about 30 percent of people with phantom limb pain and typically the phantom shrinks, rather than elongates.

Phantom limb pain has frustrated practitioners and patients for centuries. Some of the most well-known writings about phantom limb pain came from Silas Weir Mitchell, a prominent Philadelphia physician, who treated hundreds of soldiers in the Civil War. Injuries to limbs in the Civil War era often resulted in infection and gangrene since antibiotics had not yet been discovered. Removal of the limb was often the only option. Those who did live through the process (and what a process!) were often left with pain in the limb that was removed. Dr. Mitchell was the first to describe the condition as "phantom limb pain." Treatment possibilities and a greater understanding of this disorder did not happen for many decades after Dr. Mitchell first coined the term.

Trying to make sense of phantom pain using the old model of pain (that it is a beneficent warning of impending damage), healthcare providers generally had two options to explain it. First, the pain exists due to an injury to the nerve that could not be seen. Secondly (here we go again), the patient is ultimately to blame because the pain is psychogenic due to the traumatic loss of limb.

To address the possibility of damage to the nerve at the site of amputation, doctors attempted re-severing the nerve to start anew. In some cases, this was done multiple times at higher and higher sections, all the way to the spinal cord itself. Sadly, the patients experienced no change in the pain experience.

The success rate of surgical interventions or the use of drug therapy in phantom limb pain is at maximum about 30 percent.

While there certainly might be some cases of nerve injury during the traumatic accident that preceded the amputation, the concept of nerve injury as the source of phantom pain is called into question when people who were born without a limb also have phantom limb sensations. These unfortunate individuals have sensations in an arm that they have never physically possessed. They feel the missing limb as quite real, as though there is a shadow image of the limb in the brain. The fact that these people "feel" the phantom arm suggests that there is some hard-wired representation of each limb in the brain. If there is a representation of the limb in the brain, there is also a possibility to experience pain.

A huge leap in the understanding of phantom limb pain came through the work of Vilayanur S. Ramachandran, a behavioral neurologist. (Who knew there were such professions?) Dr. Ramachandran is an insightful thinker, the kind of person who changes the way a generation of scientists thinks about an issue. His pioneering work, like all other scientific breakthroughs, was based on insights gained from the groundwork laid by other scientists who preceded him.

The first piece of the puzzle was laid by Dr. Wilder Penfield (1891–1976), a neurosurgeon in Montreal specializing in epilepsy. Dr. Penfield had studied with the finest teachers of his day, Sir William Osler and Sir Charles Scott Sherrington, while a student at Oxford University. In the 1930s, Dr. Penfield published a paper on work he had done during open skull surgeries. While undergoing brain surgery, the patient remained fully conscious and communicative while Dr. Penfield stimulated parts of his/her brain with an electric probe. Dr. Penfield discovered that specific parts of the brain triggered sensation to specific parts of the body. Over time, Dr. Penfield developed a map of these areas, which became known as the "Penfield homunculus."

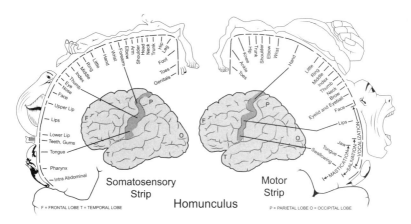

Figure 10.1: The Penfield homunculus

After decades of doing these surgeries, Penfield discovered that the map is quite consistent from person to person. He used an electrode to stimulate a certain point at the site and the patient would report feeling sensation in a corresponding body area. Since Dr. Penfield was exploring epilepsy, he never thought to explore this question: *what happens to the homunculus if the bodily region represented is missing?*

This question did, however, cross the mind of Michael Merzenich, a researcher who explored Dr. Penfield's ideas. The research methodology had become much more specific: the electrodes used by Merzenich were much smaller than those of Penfield, making the map much clearer and more detailed. Merzenich studied the effect on the homunculus of a monkey when the nerves to a limb were completely severed. He found that the brain remapped the area that is supposed to have sensory information coming from the limb. Since the nerve to the limb was severed, this is essentially the same as amputation, rather like a neural amputation than a removal of the limb itself. This remapping of the brain conflicted with a long-held belief that the connections in the brain are hard-wired and not subject to change. This hard-wired concept of the brain began in 1919 through the writings of Dr. Santiago Ramon y Cajal, who won the 1906 Nobel Prize for Medicine. Merzenich's findings clearly conflicted with a long-held and accepted truth of neurology. Instead of going dormant, the areas that correlated to a specific area were filled in by adjacent areas of the brain. The brain used the available unused space for regions that were still active. It is a bit like seeing an empty lot next to your house consistently vacant; pretty soon you start using it for your own activities since no one else is occupying it.

Dr. Tim Pons at the National Institute for Mental Health was able to study Merzenich's research monkeys years after the original experiments. People for the Ethical Treatment of Animals (PETA) had these monkeys seized in 1981 and Pons got word that several of them had grown old and were about to be euthanized. He convinced the National Institute for Mental Health to allow him to study these monkeys to see what happened to their brains after years of having the nerves to a limb severed. What Pons discovered is that adjacent areas of the brain map had occupied the area of the missing limb. Merzenich had found that the brain reorganized from a distance of 1–2 millimeters; Pons found that the reorganization was as broad as 14 millimeters, a huge distance in the brain. If you look at the homunculus, it can be seen that the area that corresponds to the face is next to that of the hands and fingers. When Pons stimulated the area of the face, neurons connected with the hand began to fire.

Dr. Ramachandran, after reading the work of Dr. Pons, decided to explore this in people with phantom pain. Sure enough, stroking specific areas of the face with a Q-tip produced sensations in the phantom limb of one of his patients. This was replicated time and time again, confirming the reality of the neural reorganization and presenting a possible explanation for phantom limb pain in general. Even though the nerves are severed, the region of the brain connected to that area is still active and is capable of reorganization. Not unlike the phenomenon of referred pain, the brain can mislocalize where the sensation is originating. Remarkably, the sensation experienced was quite specific: a brush on the face felt like a brush across the phantom arm; painful stimulus on the face was felt as painful stimulation to the phantom arm. This correlation of sensations then leads to the following question: if there is no painful stimulus applied to the represented area in the brain, why is the phantom limb experiencing pain?

One explanation for the experience of pain lies in what neuroscientists call the brain's "best guess" phenomenon. For missing limbs, consider the following scenario. My 90-year-old mother lives alone about two hours away. Suppose I call her on the phone and there is no answer. There are a number of benign explanations for that, which I probably consider first. The more times my calls go unanswered, however, the more likely I am to believe that something is seriously wrong, perhaps even calling the police to check on her. One possible explanation for phantom pain is much the same: if there is no information for an extended period of time, something must be seriously wrong. If something is seriously wrong in the body, there is usually pain involved. Like an alarm system in a house, cutting a wire to a sensor eliminates the input from that particular zone. Sensing no input, the central alarm system assumes the worst, that something must be wrong and therefore dangerous. The brain also supposes that something is terribly amiss with the limb and uses the experience of pain to sound the alarm.

The phantom limb story takes a very interesting turn due to Dr. Ramachandran's training both as a medical doctor and as a visual researcher. His medical training was in India where being pragmatic and innovative with precious resources was a distinct advantage. Even now, as a famous researcher who has access to a staggering array of technology, he prefers to use the simplest of tools coupled with critical thinking skills.

Drawing on his understanding of visual phenomena, Ramachandran wondered what would happen to the patient if he/she could "see" a limb where there is none, using a box with multiple mirrors. The reflection of the existing arm would create the illusion of the presence of an arm on the other side of the body. When he tried this, the results were astonishing. In many people, the illusion of seeing the missing limb completely resolved the phantom pain. One of the most startling (and puzzling) aspects of the mirror box is that the patient is fully aware that the reflected arm is not real. Even knowing this, visually seeing the reflection often resolves the phantom limb pain. This is not dissimilar to a magician creating an illusion to fool him/herself and yet still believing the illusion. This approach has been used with excellent results by many clinicians since the publishing of Dr. Ramachandran's (with co-author Sandra Blakeslee) excellent book called *Phantoms in the Brain* in 1998.

How is it possible that Dr. Ramachadran's simple approach using an arrangement of mirrors has such a powerful effect? Numerous studies in what is called motor imagery have proved that when the brain imagines moving an arm, the neural mechanisms that create that movement fire. Close your eyes and imagine looking over your right shoulder (without actually moving your neck). All the muscles that contract to create right rotation of the neck spike in activity, just from you imagining the movement. Giraux and Sirigu (2003) used just that principle to treat people with phantom limb pain. Instead of using mirrors, they had subjects vividly imagine moving the phantom limb. As the person sees an arm moving on a computer screen and imagines moving the phantom arm, there is seemingly some harmonization of the motor aspect of the brain with the visual experience.

These experiments are also being pursued with virtual reality setups which can create amazing illusions of the phantom limb. The experiments may also be able to link neural signals with the movement, making the movement exactly linked to the brain. Of course, virtual reality labs such as this are substantially more expensive than Dr. Ramachandran's simple mirror box and may not be, for the time being, clinically useful. As the cost of this technology decreases, however, we may see it becoming more widely available.

Another possible area of phantom limb treatment lies in increasing the perceptual acuity of sensory processing in the brain. Since the brain's sensory processing from the missing limb has been altered and the brain is trying to make sense of this new reality, it is quite possible that the nerves in the tissue of the stump are not giving the brain accurate sensory information. The clearer the picture the brain receives, the more appropriate the response can be.

To develop better sensory skills, a therapist might touch the stump repeatedly with various kinds of inputs such as a brush, something sharp, cold, warm, etc. Using fine-pointed objects, he/she may train the patient to perceive point discrimination by asking him/her to perceive how many points of contact are being made with each object. Helping the person to discriminate one sensation from the other helps to rewire the sensory cortex based on *current* information, not *historical* information. This also has been shown to help reduce phantom pain.

The lessons learned from phantom pain translate across the full spectrum of the experience of pain. A new understanding of the brain's internal map of the body can help us to understand that pain, even though it cannot be seen, is very real. Can you imagine the feelings of some amputees who were told by healthcare providers that the pain they felt in the non-existent limb was psychological? In some cases, patients were told they manifested a desire to feel something, anything, in the limb. How must these patients feel while reading the work of Ramachandran and colleagues?

I would think that the lesson for all healthcare providers is in learning to observe, without judgment, when a person relays his/her experience of pain. A deep model of understanding, based on solid science, can help make the seemingly random presentation of symptoms understandable and explainable. As explored earlier in the chapter on meaning and context, helping the pain sufferer to understand the context of symptoms can significantly ease pain and suffering. Patients deserve nothing less.

CHAPTER 11

TRIGGER POINTS AND REFERRED PAIN

An action over here, an effect over there…

> Myofascial Trigger Point: A hyper-irritable spot, usually within a taut band of skeletal muscle or in the muscle's fascia. The spot is painful on compression and can give rise to characteristic referred pain, tenderness, and autonomic phenomena.
>
> Travell and Simons 1992, p.4

Of all the possible reasons why we may experience pain, the most common is pain due to musculoskeletal causes. Even so, musculoskeletal pain is often overlooked because it is often moderate in nature and less urgent than pain from other maladies. But while it may (but not always) be less on the intensity scale, musculoskeletal pain is extremely high on the prevalence scale. Estimates are that, at any one time, as much as 40 percent of the population is in pain. Given the huge numbers of people affected, musculoskeletal pain is a very important piece of the pain experience.

With this kind of prevalence, one would think that more resources would be available for musculoskeletal problems, especially those of a muscular nature. One of my personal mentors and heroes, the late Dr. David Simons, called muscles the orphan organ, where no one profession makes them their specialty. There was a time, in my youth and bravado, I really felt like a pioneer in a new field, trying to help those who were not served by mainstream medicine.

Age and experience often changes perception. The longer I have been in the field, the more I have seen things from a different perspective. First, this isn't a new field. Second, there is good reason why few healthcare providers make soft-tissue pain their specialty. This is not an accident. Soft-tissue pain is messy, the boundaries are seriously blurred, and there are few simple answers. You must be seriously committed to the field to deal with the challenges. I was many years in the field before I grasped the complexity of the task I had chosen. I really didn't know how difficult, yet how valuable, the field of manual therapy is. I hope to share that with you in this chapter.

There are many categories of muscular pain such as tears, strains, and soreness from chemical issues such as nutritional deficits or drug interactions. The list is long and daunting. In this chapter, we focus on one specific and often overlooked source, referred pain from myofascial trigger points. The subject of referred pain is a perfect addition to the mystery of pain; referred pain is complex and nothing is as it seems to be. Patient and practitioner alike have been fooled by referred pain and trigger points, and knowledge of their presence can help thousands struggling with unexplained pain. Ignorance of trigger point phenomena can have you thinking the worst about your pain, not realizing there just might be an answer.

The history of trigger points

The most well-known pioneer in the field of trigger point therapy is the American physician Janet Travell (1901–1997). Dr. Travell was exposed to the trigger point literature from writings in Germany and England, probably also in no small part because her father was a physician who dealt with musculoskeletal pain. She also became the White House Physician to President John F. Kennedy, helping him deal with his numerous musculoskeletal problems. Her extensive writings and research have left the world a treasury of knowledge that has helped people ever since. As in any other field, the most articulate spokesperson is often standing on the shoulders of others who came before.

People have had muscular aches and pain through the ages. Every system of healing has had some sort of approach to muscular discomfort. In Europe in the 1800s, there was widespread use of the term rheumatism to describe muscular aching and discomfort. Unfortunately, this term covered too many physical conditions (such as rheumatic fever) and later was clarified as muscular rheumatism. Remember when rheumatism was a much more commonly used term than arthritis?

Perhaps one of the first to write about finding nodules in the muscle tissue of patients in pain was William Balfour, an Edinburgh physician. The nineteenth-century Dutch physician Johan Mexger, Swedish physician Uno Helleday in 1876, and a German doctor named Strauss (1898) all wrote about abnormalities in muscle tissue. I was somewhat amused to read that a German doctor named Müller stated that these nodules are seldom discovered because finding them takes skill and patience. He believed doctors were not looking for them in an organized manner, and thus those poorly trained doctors doubted the existence of such points. That was 1912!

Physicians in the 1800s began to notice how areas of focal tenderness could refer discomfort elsewhere. In 1841, a French physician called these nodules "les points douloureux" (painful points) and noted how they referred pain to other areas. Perhaps the greatest body of work, which then influenced Dr. Janet Travell, came from the work of Dr. John Kellgren. Dr. Kellgren injected the connective tissue and muscles of healthy people with small amounts of saline solution, producing referred pain and sensation. Perhaps most importantly, these referral patterns were remarkably similar from subject to subject. Injections in the same spot in multiple people produced referred sensations that were predictable and reproducible.

Dr. Kellgren's work was extremely important as it demonstrated a previously unexplained phenomenon (referred sensation). The idea that one muscle could refer sensation (I can't simply use the term pain, because often trigger points refer other sensations, such as burning, nerve-like sensations, itching, etc.) to other muscles was a radically new concept. Dr. Kellgren also pointed out that muscles don't just refer to other muscles; they may refer to a joint, mimicking pain that might be mistaken for arthritis. They could, as in the case of the temporalis muscle, refer pain to a specific tooth. This condition would surely have been mistaken for a dental problem, which still happens today.

It is remarkable how some discoveries land in fertile soil and others fall onto deaf ears. What if Copernicus had been born one hundred years later and had the updraft of the Renaissance under his wings? What if Michael Merzenich, one of the pioneers of the idea of neuroplasticity, presented his papers 20 years later? Instead of being ridiculed out of a scientific conference, he might have been heralded for opening the eyes of the scientific community. Instead, it seems early scientific pioneers are destined to plant their seeds on very rocky soil, soil which rejects their ideas because the cause is thought to be already known. (Einstein said, "That which holds us back isn't what we do not know, it is what we think we know.") Kellgren's ideas came at a time in which the prevailing wisdom was that most muscular pain is really a manifestation of emotional turmoil. From the lack of available diagnostic testing, doctors could find no other explanation. Not knowing precise physical examination techniques that verified a clear organic cause for pain, doctors assumed that the pain is really psychogenic.

At this point of the trigger point story, enter the aforementioned Dr. Janet Travell. Dr. Travell was motivated with an insatiable desire to learn, a sincere desire to help her patients, and also because she too suffered with pain. Pressing into her own muscle tissue, she was able to replicate and intensify her symptoms, like, as she says, "turning on an electrical switch." What followed was a prolific career of research and clinical practice into these trigger point areas. She and Dr. David Simons wrote the definitive book on trigger points called *Myofascial Pain and Dysfunction: The Trigger Point Manual* in 1983. It is a wealth of information for healthcare providers who treat musculoskeletal pain.

It is important to remember that trigger points are extremely small. As the phrase trigger point has become more commonly used, it has been used to describe any area of restriction and sensitivity in a muscle. People think of a golf-ball sized knot in a muscle as a trigger point. In reality, true trigger points within a muscle are tiny nodular areas about the size of a grain of rice. One negative result of their diminutive size is that finding a trigger point takes skill and training, not something done without guidance. While they can be self-treated or treated by loved ones and family, some knowledge is necessary to know what you are looking for.

Trigger points are located in a tight band of tissue, appropriately called a taut band. These thin strands feel about the width of a piece of yarn. Somewhere along the taut band may be a nodule-like area, which is the trigger point. Finding the taut band is essential to locating the trigger point, as shown in the drawing.

TRIGGER POINT COMPLEX

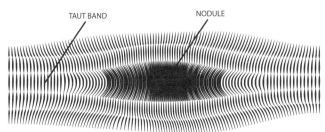

Figure 11.1: The epicenter of a trigger point feels nodule-like, due to the contraction of muscle fibres. On either side of the nodule, corresponding muscle fibres are pulled taut.

Qualities of a trigger point

Sensitivity

One hallmark of trigger points is that they are exquisitely sensitive when pressed upon, often feeling like a piece of glass embedded in the tissue. When as a therapist I press on a trigger point, the person often perceives that I am pressing with great force, when in reality the pressure is often quite light. For comparison, I often go to the other side of the body or move to a different area in the same muscle to show them the sensitivity difference. Three or four times the pressure in the healthy area is needed to create the same discomfort. Since people often find this hard to believe, I use an instrument that measures the exact application of pressure. People are astounded at how sensitive one specific area is, but the trick is that the trigger point, being small, is easy to miss. Moving as much as 5mm away will put the therapist completely off the mark. Specificity is absolutely everything. It isn't about the pressure used, it's about the exactness of the location. Another way to look at this is that being less than 1cm off the mark is the difference between success and failure. This is an exacting science.

Muscles are a collection of many smaller components called sarcomeres, overlapping strands that are brought together to create a muscle contraction. In a trigger point, some of those strands have compressed together (contracted) and stay closed (contracture). Since these contracted areas are part of a larger strand, the area outside of the contracted area is now pulled taut, which makes it easy to feel when the examiner pulls a finger across the taut band of tissue. Not every taut band has a trigger point, but every trigger point is housed in a taut band.

Jump sign or local twitch response

When a trigger point is pressed, it is often surprisingly tender. This tenderness comes from neural hypersensitivity. When the therapist contacts the trigger point, there is often a reflexive jump or twitch, as the point is hypersensitive to stimulation. These twitch responses are clearly seen when the trigger point is contacted with a needle, such as an acupuncture needle. Sometimes, it is also possible to do this with finger pressure. More often, the reaction of the person is also called a "jump and shout" response.

The most important criterion of all is the recipient's recognition of the sensation referred from the trigger point. Whenever I think of this, I always remember my first meeting with Dr. Simons. I asked him in a long and far too elaborate way how a therapist might confirm the area being treated is truly the source of the patient's pain. He kindly looked me in the eye and said, "The patient will tell you."

Replication of symptoms

This simple rule is vitally important. The hallmark of success for the treatment of trigger points is replication of symptoms. When you press on a specific point and the person says, "That's my pain," you have found the place you are looking for. It doesn't take patient education or salesmanship to convince the recipient that the spot you are pressing upon is connected to the pain. If the presenting pain is a headache that feels like it is behind the eye, a specific point in a muscle in the back of the neck can re-create that pain behind the eye perfectly. I push, the eye headache intensifies. I let up on the trigger point and the pain disappears. The relationship between my pressure and the headache is obvious.

In the simplest of terms, this is the essence of trigger point therapy. In many ways, I have felt lucky to be involved in a field where the connections are so immediately apparent. Think of the leap of faith that must happen with approaches such as medicine or acupuncture. I put a needle here and it will affect your liver. Take this little pill and it will make your toe hurt less.

These are leaps that we don't think about because we have been educated.

> When I think of this, I always think about my experience teaching Precision Neuromuscular Therapy in the mountains of El Salvador. I was teaching the community members how to treat each other (they have little to no healthcare), and that particular afternoon I was treating people from the community.
>
> Glancing up into the mountain-side, I saw a figure come into a clearing. My translator predicted that this man was probably coming to see me, which was about a two-hour walk from that clearing. Sure enough, two hours later, this man appeared. As we greeted him, he asked if we had medicine. "No," the translator said, "Mr. Nelson treats with his hands, not with pills." The man graciously thanked us and turned to begin his walk home, leaving me stunned and speechless. In this the most remote of places, there is still a belief that only medicine can help. It was a moment I will never forget.

Referred sensation: Still a mystery!

The hallmark of trigger points is their ability to refer sensation to other parts of the body. Like a gun, a relatively small action in one place (pulling the trigger) creates a powerful response in a distant location (damage from the bullet). While most of the time the sensation is a deep aching pain, it can be numerous other sensations as well. Trigger points can mimic the tingling and numbness of nerve pain so perfectly that I doubt anyone would discern the difference between true nerve issues and trigger point referral by the quality of the sensation alone. As someone who is supposed to be knowledgeable about trigger points, I too have been fooled more than once into thinking

I had a neural entrapment issue, only to discover later it was a trigger point.

Trigger points can also create powerful autonomic sensations, like a feeling of immediate nausea. When the therapist presses the offending trigger point, it feels like the reaction goes straight to the gut. Sometimes the sensation is not nausea but an immediate outbreak of sweating, goose-bumps, or watering of the eye. The person is often incredulous at the experience, finding it hard to believe a muscular trigger point could do that.

Another referred sensation which is not in the category of pain has come up many times in my years of practice: that of tinnitus, the sensation of ringing in the ears. Tinnitus is a frustrating experience; the ringing is almost always present in the background, to varying volumes depending on the severity of the condition. There are many possible causes of tinnitus, the most common being long-term exposure to loud noises. Exposure to loud noises would generally affect both ears equally. However, with musculoskeletal causes, it is more likely that the ringing will be on one side only. This is an important diagnostic clue. I vividly remember one woman who could alter her ringing by moving her jaw in a specific position, which implied that the source of her pain might very well be due to a trigger point, since movement and position made such a difference. When I touched a trigger point in one of the muscles of her jaw, it immediately lessened the ringing, which completely stopped after three treatments. A further clue to the trigger point being the source of her tinnitus is that the ringing started after an automobile accident.

Another aspect of trigger points is their ability to create reflex activity (tension) in another muscle. In the simplest terms, one would think that a trigger point in a muscle would increase the tension only in the muscle in which the trigger point resides. You may have heard the phrase *pain-spasm-pain cycle*. In this concept, a muscle has a problem (injury), tightens in response to the pain, which then produces more pain, which produces more spasm, etc. This idea has circulated for many decades and is often taught in every discipline of healthcare. Unfortunately, the science does not support this concept.

Muscles have essentially one job, which is to contract. Under duress, they are not going to perform the same amount of work as when they are healthy and at full capacity. If there is a problem (i.e. trigger point), the tendency is to do less activity, because the capability is less. Think of it this way: if you feel terrible or compromised in some way, you do not increase your activity level, you lessen it. Muscles with lessened activity present as weak. Weakness as a result of a trigger point is called motor inhibition. Since muscles work in groups, other muscles with similar jobs to the weakened muscle must be recruited to perform the action. Those muscles in that functional group now work much harder because of the presence of a trigger point in a muscle in their group. As a result, the pain-spasm-pain cycle isn't *that* far off: muscles that do the same job as the injured muscle have to increase their workload to compensate for the injured muscle, which often then leads to pain.

A note about weakness

If you see your doctor about persistent shoulder pain, he/she may refer you to a physical therapist for evaluation. The therapist is likely to strength test all the muscles of the shoulder and there is a good chance of finding one or two muscles quite weak. Since motor inhibition from a trigger point will present as weakness, this presents an inherent problem. If your muscle is weak because of a trigger point, any effort to strengthen the muscle will further overload an already compromised muscle. As a result, you will probably experience more pain than before the therapy. For a while, you may put up with the increase in pain, but that probably won't last very long. You start backing off the exercise, which lessens the pain. The therapist, however, starts questioning your commitment to the healing process and encourages you to push on. The more you exercise that muscle, the more pain you endure. Sound familiar? Weakness that is a result of motor inhibition from a trigger point must be distinguished from true weakness. Similarly, muscle tension may be local or referred. No one knows why some trigger points refer increased activity (spasm) to other muscles and other trigger points refer inhibition (weakness). Both must be investigated.

Internal organs are another possible source of referred pain, one that primary care physicians are very familiar with. Each organ has very specific patterns of referral, such as the gall bladder referring pain under the right shoulder blade. When describing your pain to a doctor, chances are he/she is thinking about what organ system would create those particular symptoms. Location of pain alone is not definitive; you must have other accompanying symptoms (such as nausea in the case of the gall bladder) for a visceral referral to be the likely cause. Making the distinction between organ and muscular referrals is obviously crucial. In general, muscular referrals are made better or worse with movement or position. Visceral (internal organ) referrals are not movement dependent and have other associated symptoms reflective of the suspected organ.

Trigger points: The great mimics

One of the major issues that trigger points pose is their ability to mimic more serious conditions. When I speak to physician groups about trigger points, the emphasis of the presentation is usually on the potential for trigger points to mislead the best of doctors. Describing the common clinical conditions trigger points can mimic resonates for physicians, especially primary care doctors. Doctors typically rule out various catastrophic possible causes for a patient's pain. The problem is, after the catastrophic causes are ruled out, the person is still in pain. Primary care doctors get this, specialists often don't.

When a person is referred to a specialist, this physician carefully rules out possible causes in his/her area of specialty. Proudly, they announce to the patient that he/she does not have the feared condition. While not catastrophic in nature, the patient still has the original pain. The patient does not continue going to the specialist at this point; they go back to the primary care doctor for additional help. Primary physicians are often the most pragmatic doctors because the unsuccessful cases ultimately keep landing back in their offices. When I do presentations to primary care doctors about trigger points mimicking symptoms commonly seen in the clinic, faces in the room light up. Here are some common examples.

The big one

Trigger points in muscles such as the scalenes (a muscle in the front of the neck) and the levator costarum (a muscle in the back) can refer pain to the chest and down the arm. If this happens on the left side, the sufferer is likely to assume that they are in the midst of a heart attack. I would love to have statistics on the number of people who visit emergency rooms with symptoms of a heart attack who are ultimately told (after much testing) that the cause is musculoskeletal. Ideally, figuring out a safe and accurate way to explore the musculoskeletal avenue first would save a lot of money. The danger with this strategy is that we certainly do not want to overlook a serious problem, but I wonder if there is a way to be more efficient with the assessment.

I was also one of those people who went to the doctor with difficulty breathing; every deep breath I took felt like someone was stabbing me in the back and the pain went to my chest and down the left arm. At 40, I thought I was having a heart attack. The doctor asked me to breathe deeply and rotate my upper body to the right. The stabbing pain shot down my arm. He then asked me to turn to the left and breathe deeply again.

It was miraculous; I could breathe deeply with no pain as long as I was turned to the left. The doctor and I figured out quickly that it wasn't my heart, since my heart doesn't really care which way I rotate my upper body. The pain in my chest was indeed musculoskeletal. Luckily (actually, quite embarrassingly for me) I knew what to do about this, which was a trip to my own clinic to see one of my staff.

This brings us to the second problem: what happens to the people who are told that the heart is fine and the problem is simply musculoskeletal? Often, these people are given medication and sent on their way, in the hope that time will resolve the symptoms. We could probably do a better job of helping these people after they leave the emergency room by two or three accurate and effective trigger point treatments.

Too embarrassing to discuss

On more than one occasion, I have been treating someone for a problem like lower back pain and I see a look of perplexity come over his face. When I ask what is happening, he can't quite put a sentence together. It is clear that he has a question, but the client cannot, or will not, come out and say it. After some internal struggle and silence, he will inquire as to whether there is any connection between the spot I am pressing on, and "there." When it is clear I am not exactly sure where "there" is, the truth comes out. In a male, it is testicular pain. If the client is a female, she may (and this is obviously something difficult to reveal to a male) tell me about her labial pain that has taken her numerous times to the gynecologist. This pain has severely negatively impacted her life, including several unhelpful visits to physicians who are equally frustrated because they can't find a cause. For her, there is a fear that some looming disease process exists that no one has yet detected. Worse yet, the pain may cause intercourse to be painful, which has negatively affected her marriage. Here she is in the office of a therapist she does not know and this therapist can re-create her labial pain by pressing on a tender spot in her back.

For a male, the same situation can occur with testicular pain. After a few unrewarding trips to the doctor's office, it just isn't something you mention to anyone. As with the female client, pressure on a certain muscle and/or ligament in the back can re-create the testicular pain like flipping a switch to the "on" position. The client often immediately understands that the trigger point in the residing muscle and the pelvic pain are connected.

Often, I see a look of astonishment on the face of the client first, followed by frustration that he/she had lived with this pain so long when the answer was hiding in a muscle. Luckily, these problems were addressed by accident, as the muscles I was treating happen to play an important role in back pain, which is why this person was in my office. These people would never have visited my office for pelvic pain as they would never think the source was muscular in nature. How many people out there are suffering with unexplained pelvic pain that is ultimately due to the presence of trigger points?

Headaches

There are some studies that show that about 4–5 percent of the population gets more than 15 headaches a month. A month! The courage and perseverance of these headache sufferers is admirable and amazing. Again, while there are many causes of headaches, one often overlooked cause could be trigger points in the head and neck area which re-create numerous headache patterns. One muscle (the sternocleidomastoid) in the front of the neck can mimic the typical pattern of a migraine perfectly. Migraines commonly affect one side of the head with a pain pattern over the frontal area. This is exactly the area of referral from the sternocleidomastoid muscle. Since many people who have headaches have never obtained an accurate diagnosis or have been misdiagnosed, it is reasonable to assume there are thousands of people right now who suffer needlessly with what they think are migraines, but are really not.

How would you know the difference between a migraine and a trigger point headache? Migraines are a disorder of the nervous system rather than just a type of headache, but the quality of headache that results from a migraine is typically throbbing and is made worse with activity. Also, migraine headaches often have other phenomena associated with them such as auras, light sensitivity, and sound sensitivity. Typically, migraines are also episodic, lasting for 24–36 hours. If a headache has none of these qualities and lasts for days on end, one should consider the possibility that the headache is caused by trigger point activity.

I remember one young lady in her early twenties who came to me with severe headaches, so much so that she was on partial disability. Having had migraines since her teens, she was in an accident two years ago and since then had daily headaches, which were diagnosed as migraines. Her headaches were throbbing only occasionally, mostly present every day, making her life miserable. When the trigger point was deactivated, the headaches resumed in the pattern more typical for her previous to the accident—one or two migraines a month. (This was why her headaches were occasionally throbbing. She was having a migraine *on top of* her trigger point headache.) I am happy to say that she went back to work full time and resumed a normal life.

Ligaments and joints as possible sources of referred sensation

As noted earlier, muscles are not the only source of referred sensation. Ligaments may also refer sensation in fairly predictable patterns. In 1958, Dr. George Hackett experimented with the same injection techniques as Kellgren, but Hackett injected ligaments instead of muscles. Long thought to be rather inert structures, ligaments are the connective tissue bindings that hold bone to bone, such as between the vertebrae in the low back.

The prevailing wisdom at the time was that these structures are void of sensation. Hackett's idea that they are a possible source of nociception was quite revolutionary, given the prevailing perception of ligaments. When he followed the same procedure of injection as Kellgren, predictable patterns emerged. He found that each ligament had its own pattern of referral, creating another possible explanation for people in pain. While this relationship was discovered in the 1950s, it has yet to be thoroughly researched.

Perhaps better known are the possible referral patterns of the vertebral joints in the spine. If a specific joint has sensitized neural receptors, often the result of some compressive trauma or long-standing muscular shortness, the joint will create sensation elsewhere. How is this known? Exactly the same way that Kellgren investigated trigger points. Inject the vertebral joint with an irritant and people who previously had no pain will report referred pain in distant parts of the body. Each cervical joint refers to a fairly predictable area of the body, as illustrated in the chart.

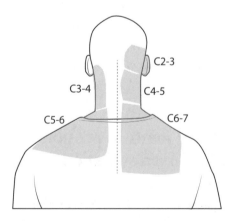

Figure 11.2: Facet referral patterns

Unfortunately, it seems that the lumbar spine, also capable of referring sensation, is not so predictable. Problems at joints in the low back may create a localized referral in the back or buttocks, or may extend down the leg mimicking sciatic pain. The problem with these joint referrals, as with most everything in this chapter, is that the source of pain cannot be seen on an imaging study. For many in healthcare, if it can't be seen, it does not exist.

How do trigger points refer sensation?

In medicine, the way a chemical such as a drug or a neurotransmitter acts on the body is called "mechanism of action." Ideally, you want to know not only what something does, but how it accomplishes the effect. To know the mechanism of action is to understand the process more deeply and possibly alter the effect along the way.

With the referred sensation of trigger points, the mechanism of action is still not well understood. There are several theories, but the bottom line is that the mechanism of action is still a mystery.

Here is the good news. At the most practical level, it is not necessary to know. The exact mechanism by which many drugs work is not completely known, yet it doesn't stop physicians from using them effectively and safely. As long as the effect is predictable and reproducible, that is valid enough.

This is exactly the argument that Dr. Travell made when the concept of referred sensation was questioned by her peers. People challenged the concept because it did not follow a known pathway such as the path of a nerve. Why should the infraspinatus muscle (a muscle in the back of the shoulder) refer to the front of the shoulder? Why there? What Dr. Travell asserted is that, scientifically, it is not necessary to know the mechanism in order to use the information to help people. If you inject an irritant into the infraspinatus muscle of pain-free subjects and the majority of them get referred pain to the front of the shoulder, this is enough to validate the existence of trigger points. How and why are for later; there are people to be helped now. She was quite correct.

It is certainly ideal to know the mechanism of referred sensation. If we understood the process, it would probably lead to a deeper understanding and ultimately better treatment techniques. As of the present, we have only some reasonable theories.

One of the most prevalent ideas is that when multiple inputs (called sensory inputs) converge on their way up the spinal column, the brain gets the source of the input mixed up or combines them. The brain essentially mislocalizes the source of the pain. There is a wonderful saying in neuroscience: that which fires together wires together. If the brain gets two simultaneous inputs, it binds them together. It is indeed possible that part of what makes trigger point treatment effective is helping the brain to uncouple the two inputs that have been intermingled.

What causes trigger points to form in the first place?

The research is still very early, but seems to point to a few potential causes in the formation of trigger points.

Overload

Trigger points are likely to form when muscles are pushed beyond their limits. The most likely way this happens is from a lengthening contraction, called eccentric contraction. Imagine bending over slowly to put a baby carefully on the bed. The muscles of your back are working very hard to control the descent of your upper body towards the bed, lengthening and contracting at the same time. Researchers think these kinds of eccentric contractions are probable causes for trigger point formation.

Another form of overload is constant contraction without rest. If one is doing an activity which requires muscle contraction, rest periods are necessary. There are certainly workplace environments where rest is not at the discretion of the worker, which can lead to serious problems. One researcher, Dr. William Staub, told me that if workers get to choose the timing of breaks and the speed of assembly, workplace injuries markedly decrease yet productivity isn't affected.

Shortened position

Muscles have a very sensitive monitoring system as to their length. If a muscle is kept in a shortened position for long periods of time, trigger points could develop. For example, consider someone who has a cast on an arm for six weeks. Once the cast is gone and full extension of the arm is finally possible, the person is horrified to discover that the muscles, which have been shortened for weeks, have now developed trigger points that won't allow full length. How frustrating is that?

Nerve root compression

If there is a compression of a nerve root in the spine, any muscle that is served by that nerve root is more likely to develop trigger points. Nerves look remarkably like the root system of a tree. Each nerve is part of a larger nerve branch that serves other muscles as well. Affect the nerve from above and everything served by that nerve branch is also affected. This probably doesn't initiate trigger point formation, but it does make the nerves along the pathway more susceptible to further insults.

True weakness

The less capacity (strength) a muscle has, the more likely it is to be pushed beyond its limits. This is why staying strong is so important, especially as we age.

Why isn't treatment more available?

There are probably three main reasons why excellent trigger point treatment is not more readily available to the general public:

1. *Time.* Manual treatment strategies take a fair amount of time to execute and they are administered on a one-to-one basis. Time is not something that most of the providers in our healthcare system have with their patients.

2. *Skill.* Because of the nature of the manual treatments, effectiveness is almost completely dependent on the skill level of the therapist. This variability in skill level is a major problem for healthcare providers and insurance companies.

3. *Imaging.* We very much prefer to treat conditions that can be seen on a diagnostic image. Imaging for trigger points is possible only in the research environment.

There are very skilled and qualified manual therapists who are adept at locating and treating trigger points. As with any discipline, there are also practicing therapists who do not have the training and expertise to be consistently effective. Do your homework and ask for recommendations from friends and colleagues as to whom to see. Don't be afraid to interview the prospective therapist to discern whether he/she has adequate training, experience, and the ability to work with you as a team.

CHAPTER 12

FIBROMYALGIA
The mystery of pain's poster child

If there was a poster child for the "mystery" aspect of pain, fibromyalgia syndrome (FMS) is it. FMS represents much of what makes chronic pain so difficult for patient and practitioner alike. Fibromyalgia went unrecognized as a condition for years, only to be subsequently over-diagnosed, which resulted in having the validity of the condition questioned again. It is a telling and sad story and a window into the world of pain.

The word fibromyalgia comes from the roots *fibro* (connective tissue), *myo* (muscle), and *algia* (pain). Fibromyalgia is a painful disorder characterized by widespread pain that has been present for more than three months. People with fibromyalgia suffer physically, mentally, and socially. Physically, they endure unceasing physical pain, much like the kind of soreness one experiences during the onset of the flu. Mentally, they experience a loss of memory and concentration capabilities. Socially, they are often isolated. Since flare-ups of symptoms are so unpredictable, they often do not attempt to commit to social activities. Worse yet, since family and friends may not understand FMS, the sufferer often is reluctant to share his/her feelings with others.

Fibromyalgia was formally recognized as a true medical condition only fairly recently, first recognized as a syndrome and disorder by the American Medical Association in 1987. Subsequently in 1990, the American College of Rheumatology (ACR) put forth their classification criteria for FMS. The World

Health Organization declared fibromyalgia as an officially recognized syndrome in 1993. In reality, of course, fibromyalgia syndrome had been around for many years before that, making life miserable for the people who had the syndrome but had no idea what it was.

The hallmark characteristics of FMS are widespread aching and muscular pain. An American College of Rheumatology (ACR) study (Wolfe *et al.* 1990) found widespread pain in 97.6 percent of all patients with fibromyalgia. The ACR also estimates that about three percent of the population suffers from FMS. People who suffer with this disorder have the same muscular achiness that precedes the flu or is the result of excessive exercise. As opposed to Myofascial Pain Syndrome, where trigger points refer pain to other areas, fibromyalgia sufferers have tender points. Tender points are areas of tissue that are hypersensitive to pressure but do not refer to other areas of the body the way that trigger points do. Trigger points can be the *cause* of pain, whereas tender points are the *result* of the disorder. When muscles are overly sensitive, they respond to moderate amounts of pressure as painful. The name for this hypersensitivity to touch is allodynia.

In FMS, the presence of allodynia in multiple areas is one of the most important criteria for diagnosis. The ACR has a very clear pattern of 18 areas of the body that are pressed upon looking for hypersensitivity to touch. If 11 or more of the 18 areas are hypersensitive, a diagnosis of FMS is given, as long as the pain has been present for more than three months.

The tender point examination

The diagrams show the locations for the 18 tender points to be evaluated. For the presence of FMS, at least 11 of the 18 must be present.

Unfortunately, at this time there is no other clinically accessible gold standard such as an imaging study or blood test that will confirm the diagnosis of FMS. These tender points and selected additional symptoms are all that physicians have to make a diagnosis. This, of course, can lead to problems.

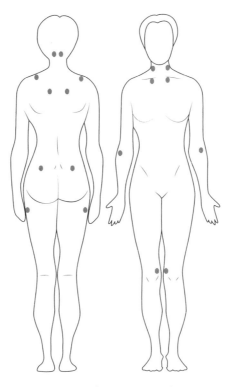

Figure 12.1: The locations of the 18 tender points examined for fibromyalgia

It's all in a name

From reading the literature, it is clear that this syndrome we now call fibromyalgia has been around for many decades. The people who struggled early on with this condition suffered in two ways. First, they had to endure the physical pain that FMS produces, which alone is a very hard burden to bear. Second, they had to endure the invalidation of their condition from the medical profession and often from their own families. Physicians, not knowing what to do with these patients, often assumed that the problem was emotionally based and sent them to psychologists. Because depression is a common co-existing condition to chronic pain, many people thought these sufferers were in pain as a result of their depression. Family members often gave little sympathy, frequently running out of patience when no solution could be found. Since no doctor could find any clear physical cause, the rest of the family secretly wished the sufferer would just snap out of it.

Further complicating this sad situation was gender bias. Since the majority of FMS patients are female, this opens the door for gender issues and biases that are potentially problematic and often devastating. There is a long history of treating women in pain differently from their male counterparts. The word hysterical has a Latin root *hystera*, which means womb. This prejudice, eloquently described in other texts, has often encouraged physicians to interpret women's experience of chronic pain as a sign of emotional upset or imbalance. Sadly, a man describing the same symptoms is not treated in the same way.

Treatment

Physicians and patients alike were often frustrated that medicines that traditionally have helped people with pain do not work for FMS. Typically, the administration of an opioid such as morphine, Oxycontin, or Darvocet is a powerful antidote to pain. In FMS, however, these medicines seem to be of little use. Researchers led by Richard Harris (Harris *et al.* 2007) discovered that key areas of the FMS brain, like the amygdala, nucleus accumbens, and the anterior cingulate do not seem to have the receptors necessary to utilize opioids.

This may also explain another aspect of FMS, that of post-exercise soreness. Typically, when people exercise, the brain dampens the pain mechanism, an effect called descending inhibition. In people with FMS, this dampening of pain during continuous exercise does not seem to work. As a result, many people with FMS are very reluctant to exercise and are often very deconditioned as a result. With their microcirculation already decreased by the condition itself, exercise could be important for health, since exercise is the best way to increase circulation. It is hard to exercise, however, if one pays such a heavy price in pain afterwards. It often takes the FMS sufferer many days to recover from post-exercise soreness.

Other common symptoms with FMS

Fatigue

Fatigue is perhaps the most common and disruptive symptom of FMS. Anyone who suffers unrelenting pain will eventually wear down from the struggle to keep up with activities of daily living. While the rest of us wrestle with the busyness of life, the FMS sufferer has to accomplish this while being in unrelenting pain. This is no small task. Many FMS sufferers describe having short periods of time where the symptoms are less, often in the middle of the day. During the rest of the day, the sufferer is quite fatigued, often having to be very selective about which tasks of daily living get accomplished. Over-exertion will often produce an increase in symptoms for days.

Sleep disorders

There is a very interesting relationship with FMS and sleep disturbances. If you deprive someone of sleep, especially the slow wave part of the sleep cycle (the most restorative), you can produce a set of symptoms almost identical to FMS. At that point, researchers thought that they had reached the Holy Grail in solving FMS. Strangely, while you can produce the symptoms through lack of quality sleep, sleep intervention alone has never proven significantly helpful to FMS. This revelation was extremely disappointing to the research community. That said, improving the quality of sleep does *help* FMS, it just isn't *the* answer.

In research done by Moldofsky (2002), researchers administered noxious stimuli into the muscles of people during deep slow-wave sleep. This resulted in the subjects transitioning out of slow-wave (restorative) sleep to the alpha and beta stages of sleep, which are much lighter and much less restorative. It seems that people with FMS have a similar circumstance: they cannot stay in the deeper sleep cycle for as long as needed. When they are in deeper sleep, the brain activity changes from delta (slow-wave, deep sleep) back to alpha waves, which are more akin to the sleep state you experience before waking.

It seems clear that resolving sleep disturbances can help lessen the pain of FMS. Many of the medicines that help FMS, such as Amitriptyline, do so at least in part because of their ability to enable more restful sleep. While sleep problems and FMS are linked, the principle should apply to all pain syndromes as well. The more restful and abundant sleep is, the more pain typically lessens.

Irritable Bowel Syndrome (IBS)

There is abundant clinical evidence that many people with FMS also have IBS. While many people who have FMS have an irritable bowel, it doesn't necessary go the other way around. The two conditions often co-exist, but they are also different in their own right. In fact, in one study (Chang *et al.* 2000), researchers discovered that the patients with FMS and IBS were hyperalgesic (over-sensitive to stimuli normally painful) while the patients with IBS alone were hypoalgesic (meaning they had reduced sensitivity to what should be regarded as pain).

IBS is often thought to be an overactivity of the sympathetic nervous system, the part of the nervous system activated during stress. (The counterpart to the sympathetic nervous system is the parasympathetic nervous system, the calming/restorative side of the nervous system.) During stress, energy is diverted to flee or fight. Anything related to restoration such as digestion is inhibited. You don't need to digest lunch if you are going to *be* lunch. Moreover, if the system is flooded with sympathetic activity, you are probably preparing to run for your life. The extra weight in your bowels is a liability, so you evacuate. This happens to all animals; getting the crap scared out of you isn't just an expression, it is a biological fact! In IBS, the process is out of control and the system keeps re-activating itself.

Loss of cognition (fibro-fog)

In surveys of people with fibromyalgia, diminished mental functioning is a commonly experienced symptom. People with FMS often struggle with memory issues, such as being unable to recall a name or the location of an object. (An interesting 2012 study by Frank Leavitt and Robert S. Katz confirmed that people with fibromyalgia have a slower word naming speed and word generation.) Some fibromyalgia sufferers even note finding driving difficult in both rapid decision-making and recall. It should be noted that these FMS sufferers have the ability to compare their present mental acuity to their pre-fibromyalgia capability, noting a sharp decline after the onset of FMS.

Migraine

There is some evidence that many people with FMS also suffer from migraines. This is actually a window into a much deeper aspect of both conditions that has to do with overactivity of the nervous system. Once we explore the process, the similarities between these conditions will make much more sense.

The symptoms of migraine, beyond the presence of a headache, are things like sensitivity to light and sound, sensitivity to any strong stimuli, and even to touch. These same symptoms can also be present in FMS. People with migraines are very sensitive to loud noises, often relegating themselves to a quiet place during the course of a migraine. Interestingly, people with FMS are also hypersensitive to sound, according to research (American Pain Society 2008). People with migraines often have cold hands; people with FMS are also very sensitive to cold in the extremities. As noted earlier, IBS is common in conjunction with FMS; people who have IBS get migraines about 60 percent more often than the general public. Sleep issues are known to affect migraines and, as discussed earlier, sleep issues are also common in FMS. Depression is also more common in both conditions relative to healthy normal individuals.

What is common to both migraines and FMS is hyper-excitation of the nervous system. In migraines, research is zeroing in on cortical spreading depression, first discovered by a Brazilian neurologist named Aristides Leao in the 1940s. The area of excitation seems to start in the brainstem, home to two very important structures in the pain experience, the locus coeruleus and the trigeminal nucleus caudalis. Both of these structures play an important role in the processing of pain. There is ample evidence that these and other parts of the brainstem play a role in FMS also.

Another interesting connection between migraines and FMS is the role of the upper cervical area of the spine. The upper cervical role in headaches is well known: compression of the spinal cord in the upper cervical area is now also an area of interest for researchers in FMS. There is also evidence to suggest that FMS can occur as a result of a cervical spine injury, such as whiplash. Buskila *et al.* (1997) found that FMS was 13 times more frequent following an injury to the neck than in the control subjects, who suffered injuries to the lower extremities.

Earlier in this chapter, I stated that there is no gold standard that will confirm the diagnosis of FMS. Given the very nature of the name, fibromyalgia, the pain that people feel is predominantly musculoskeletal. Not surprisingly, that is also where the tests have been focused, looking for some disruption in the muscular or connective tissue. More promising work is looking at disruption at the brain, which supports the idea that FMS originates from the brain downward (centrally mediated), not from the periphery up (peripherally mediated). Researchers in France (Guedji *et al.* 2008) were able to see differences in blood flow to parts of the brain that deal with pain processing by using single photon emission computed tomography (SPECT).

In both FMS and migraines, for perhaps different reasons, the nervous system goes into central sensitization, described in a previous chapter ("When the System Goes Awry"). Once this central sensitization occurs, neural activity streams down from the central nervous system to the periphery. One of the hallmarks of FMS is that the pain is bilateral: both arms, both hips, both legs, etc. One does not get FMS of the left elbow. This makes perfect sense if FMS originates from the central nervous system (CNS). If the source comes from above, the hyper-activity that results will stream down the system below in equal proportions.

The model for this might look as shown in the diagram.

This also sheds light on trigger point/tender point differences. In FMS, tender points exist because the periphery is made hypersensitive by information coming from above. In trigger points, areas of injury located in the periphery are causative and thus send input *up* to the brain, making the CNS sensitive.

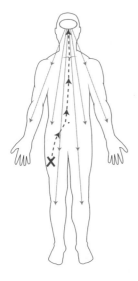

Peripheral input from a trigger point, such as this one represented in the thigh, streams additional input to the central nervous system, which in turn increases central sensitization.

Figure 12.2: The Central Sensitization model of fibromyalgia. Overactivity of the central nervous system streams increased neural activity to all of the periphery.

In FMS, as in most syndromes, the lines of demarcation are never crystal clear. There is evidence to suggest that constant peripheral input is sensitizing the CNS, even in FMS. That model may look more like as shown in the diagram.

Since problems in the peripheral tissue may further stimulate an already overactive central mechanism, peripheral treatment is a reasonable strategy. Trigger points are most likely not the source of FMS, but they can play a role in further stimulation of the CNS, which worsens the FMS. Any source of peripheral stimulation that could be reduced should be addressed, and trigger points are a powerful source. It is the sum total of all the various inputs to the CNS that creates central sensitization. Any strategy that reduces these inputs seems reasonable.

Temporal summation

People with FMS also display some very interesting characteristics of pain processing. In research by Roland Staud (2006), people with FMS were shown to process pain differently from healthy normal controls. One of these processes involves a process called wind-up, which can be altered in chronic pain conditions.

To experience the effect of wind-up, try this experiment (as was earlier described in the section on peripheral sensitization). If you have a retractable pen, click it so the ballpoint is retracted. Now, press the pen into an area on your arm with rather firm pressure, just enough to leave an impression. Now, repeat this once a second for at least a dozen times. You must hit the exact spot with the same pressure every time. What you will probably experience is that the pain gets slightly worse with each jab. Logically, this should not happen. If a certain pressure is uncomfortable the first time, it should remain at that level of discomfort each subsequent time. The response (pain) should equal the stimulus (pen poke). In reality, the pain escalates each time, to a point where it can become quite intolerable (this is like your brother punching you in the same spot on your arm time after time!).

People who have FMS experience this wind-up phenomenon differently from healthy subjects. The summation of pain (increasing sensitivity) in FMS is markedly higher. Not only does the pain increase much higher/faster from repeated stimulation but the effects also last longer. This alteration of pain processing likely points both to possible disruption in peripheral tissue and also the presence of central sensitization.

Blurred lines

One of the most frustrating aspects of fibromyalgia is establishing clear lines of symptom causation. The fibromyalgia sufferer seeks to know what specific action or event caused a spike in symptoms, but pinpointing symptoms to any particular cause is very difficult. The very nature of the syndrome, being centrally mediated (central sensitization), is at the heart of this problem. Central sensitization is a very different pain mechanism from local sensitivity. In local sensitivity, if you overuse your arms, this will likely result in pain in the muscles that were stressed. In central sensitivity, overuse of one body part may hyper-stimulate the central mechanism; the resultant pain may show up in a completely different area that was previously latent. The additional central sensitivity brings the latent area into play and that latent area may have nothing to do with the offending activity. If we think of central sensitivity like water levels, when the tide comes in, all the boats are elevated. Central mechanisms are often the sum product of collective input; it generally takes multiple influences to raise or lower the water level. Seemingly unrelated stimuli can make it worse, while lessening the input from multiple sources can decrease the level of central firing.

Adding to the confusion of causality of symptoms is the process of delayed feedback. Peripheral input (often from more than one source) goes to the brain regions, which then becomes hyper-stimulated, which will then stream a response back down the system. All this takes time, separating the offending actions from the resulting pain. The more distant cause and effect are from each other, the more difficult it is to establish a connection between the two. Therefore, it is hard to know what to do and what not to do, leading to a sense of confusion and hopelessness.

As we have seen, there are clear differences in the nervous system of the person of someone who has FMS and someone who does not. Unfortunately, the technology to detect these differences is very expensive and therefore not very practical for clinical use. As a poster child for the mystery of pain, fibromyalgia may be the leading candidate. The sufferings of those afflicted are not in alignment with observable pathology. Yet, these people are suffering indeed. There will be a day when the diagnostic technology and treatment strategies will be vastly improved and readily available. For those who have FMS, that day cannot come soon enough.

CHAPTER **13**

SOCIAL SUPPORT
AND PAIN

I am not alone…

The central theme running through this book is that the greater your understanding of pain, the more power you have to affect it positively. In this chapter, we will explore how *being understood* can be a powerful tool in reducing the devastating effects of pain. Understanding your own pain may seem to be in your control, whereas being understood may seem to be out of your control. However, there are certainly actions you can take to foster social support.

One excellent parallel is the effect of social support on individual stress. As the experience of stress goes up, the experience of pain often follows. The effect of social networks on stress has been studied by Dr. Robert Sapolsky. In his many books and articles, Dr. Sapolsky reveals insights into stress gleaned from his research with baboons. Like humans, baboons have a social network, which leads to the question: are these networks supportive or ostracizing? As you might expect, they are indeed both.

In the baboon world, quality of life hinges heavily on ranking as dominance plays a major role in their social order. Being at the bottom of the social order is not a desirable place to be, and as it turns out, not a healthy one either. Those baboons who are lowest in the social order suffer affronts from all sides. It would be easy to understand how life could be stressful for those at the very bottom of the hierarchy. Interestingly, however, it turns out that Sapolsky's research points to social connectedness as more important than social rank. Wouldn't the baboons at the top have the most connections while the baboons at the bottom have the least?

Not so, and the situation parallels our human experience. People with money and resources are not necessarily the people with deep and rich social support. In my own work with very high-level performers in sports and the arts, I have observed that being at the top can indeed be a lonely place. Often, the skill set that got you to the top requires ongoing refinement, severely limiting time for social development. Also, attaining celebrity status can totally insulate people. The cold reality is that most of the admirers who connect with you ultimately want something from you. People at the top often respond to this constant drain of energy by limiting their social network to include only old friends made long before fame came along. Alternatively, they seek out peers who could more easily relate to the struggles that come with notoriety, which is a limited group.

The same is true when looking at income and living standards. Higher levels of satisfaction/happiness and life expectancy often occur in countries that have much lower income levels. What these societies have instead of material wealth is a culture of deep social support. Cultures such as those in the Mediterranean have long been known to have longer life expectancies and the Mediterranean diet has garnered media attention for years. Perhaps it isn't just the olive oil and red wine, but the savoring of breaking bread with friends and family that makes such a difference. As Sapolsky notes, this life-expectancy discrepancy is also true within the USA. States like Vermont and Utah, which have histories of deep social networks, score highest in life expectancy. When all other variables are accounted for, it seems social networks make the difference.

The area of the brain affected by social distress is the dorsal anterior cingulate cortex (dACC), an area of the brain that we have visited numerous times in this book because of its role in the experience of pain. This area of the brain is known to light up in response to the "unpleasantness" of physical pain. In research by Naomi Eisenberger, this area of the brain is shown to light up during social distress as well. Social distress can result from many influences, but perhaps the most common is exclusion and isolation. Read what Dr. Eisenberger and Matthew Lieberman wrote in 2004:

> In an fMRI study of social exclusion participants were prevented from playing a ball-tossing game, ostensibly because of technical difficulties, in an "implicit exclusion" condition. Participants watched the others play the game without them, in what looked like exclusion, although participants consciously knew the other players were not excluding them. Nevertheless, implicit exclusion produced dACC (dorsal anterior cingulate cortex) activity indistinguishable from explicit exclusion. These studies suggest that the capacity for social exclusion to cause social pain and decrease self-esteem might be so powerful that simply viewing a scene that bears a resemblance to rejection produces these effects. Just as conscious knowledge of a visual illusion does not prevent it from occurring; conscious knowledge that one is not actually being actively excluded does not prevent dACC activity or diminished self-esteem. (Eisenberger and Lieberman 2004)

In this study, even though the subjects knew they were not being excluded by choice (explicit exclusion), they still felt the pain of exclusion in the area of the brain (dACC, the dorsal anterior cingulate cortex) that lights up during rejection and also with the unpleasantness of physical pain. The present understanding of the anterior cingulate cortex is that it activates during error detection. One of the ideas that Eisenberger and Lieberman offer is that this area of the brain could be considered a monitor for conflict detection. While this needs to be further explored,

189

it does make inherent sense. As explored in the chapter on pain and meaning, the brain wants to assign a meaning to the pain experience. If no reasonable explanation is available, there is certainly conflict. This would also be true in chronic pain syndromes, especially when the cause of the pain is not obvious.

In addition to the dACC, another part of the brain that seems to be involved in both social distress and pain is the right ventral prefrontal cortex (RVPFC). If you explore this relationship, you will find several studies on the placebo effect and the RVPFC. Even more interesting, several studies have seen spikes of activity in this area of the brain even when *thinking* about pain. (Remember the part of the IASP definition of pain that states actual or *potential* damage?) Like our subjects who knew they were not explicitly excluded from the ball-playing game, the areas of the brain linked to pain and distress lit up anyway. Wondering if those around you truly believe the extent of your pain could activate areas of the brain that sustain the pain experience.

If one area of the brain processes two separate sensations, there is a potential for spillover. (That spillover also exists in our language—we describe hurt feelings and broken hearts with the same vocabulary we use to describe broken bones and injured knees.) Eisenberger *et al.* (2006) also investigated the spillover effect. They explored two main questions: do people who are more sensitive to social distress experience more pain, and conversely, does sensitivity to physical pain relate to an individual's sensitivity to social distress? The answer to both questions seems to be yes, confirming an overlap in neural processing. What can we take from this research? One possible way to reduce the experience of physical pain is to reduce social distress, since they share neural circuitry. This has been studied in conditions such as cancer pain, pain following coronary artery bypass, and labor and delivery.

The support of a primary loved one can have a significant pain-relieving effect. In fact, the person doesn't even need to be there! Eisenberger and Master (Master *et al.* 2009) applied uncomfortable amounts of heat to the arms of willing research subjects. When subjects were looking at pictures of their significant others (with whom they had been in a relationship for more than six months), they tolerated more heat than when they were looking at a photo of someone they did not know or a picture of an object. Researchers then had the subjects hold hands with their significant other and compared that with (1) holding hands with someone they did not know and (2) compressing a squeezable stress ball. Again, the presence of someone we love was shown to have an analgesic effect on pain.

Recent research has revealed that being in love is a potent pain reducer. Dr. Sean Mackey, Arthur Aron and colleagues studied the effect of being in love on pain (Younger *et al.* 2010). Similarly to the Eisenberger and Master study previously (Master *et al.* 2009) mentioned, the researchers used pictures of loved ones which flashed on a computer screen while the subjects were administered intense heat to the forearm. The subjects were also told to bring in a picture of an acquaintance who was also visually attractive, perhaps equal to the person with whom they were in love. In this way they could compare whether the subjects benefited from the feelings associated with seeing a loved one or whether the benefit was merely one of distraction by looking at a picture of an attractive person. The researchers also decided to use pure distraction as a comparison for pain relief. Earlier studies have shown that distraction can be effective, as referenced earlier in this book. What the researchers wanted to know is whether looking at pictures of the loved one was merely a distraction or whether some other process was going on. As it turns out something else was indeed happening.

When pain is reduced by distraction, the brain centers involved are essentially cognitively based, involving the cortical centers of the brain. When a reduction in pain was shown from looking at pictures of a beloved, the part of the brain that activated is called the nucleus accumbens. This is one of the reward centers of the brain, an area that lights up during activities like gambling or during drug use. This is rather interesting considering so many people have described the initial passionate phase of love much like a drug. As it turns out, the neuroscience of love is very much like a drug. (In Younger *et al.*'s 2010 study, moderate pain was reduced by as much as 40% and severe pain by as much as 15%.)

In summary, both distraction and the initial passionate phase of love are effective in reducing pain. What is different about them is the mechanism of action. Distraction uses largely higher centers of the brain, which are involved in thinking. The mechanism of passion resides in an entirely different part of the brain which is also an effective pain reducer.

Pain and empathy

Up to this point, we have explored the relationship of pain and social relationships from the perspective of the person in pain. When the perspective is switched, the research on the effects of being in a relationship with others in pain is just as fascinating. As pain is ultimately part of life for all of us, it is also part of life for those we love. Watching a loved one suffer is indeed painful. Researchers have been exploring just how the brain responds to seeing others suffer and the results are fascinating.

In order to explore empathy, we must assume that if there is discomfort in watching another person suffer, the observer must either (1) relate the observed pain to a previous personal experience or (2) somehow take the perspective of the observed. Have you ever been talking with someone when you suddenly noticed a spider crawling on this person's body? The person to whom you are speaking is totally unaware and has not been bitten, but you have chills up and down your spine as though the spider is on you, not them. We have the ability to translate what we see into our own experience, even though it is happening to another.

This effect is due to mirror neurons, discovered quite by accident a few years ago. When Italian researchers led by Giacomo Rizzolatti (di Pellegrino *et al.* 1992; Gallese *et al.* 1996) studied the motor neurons of the Macaque monkey, they noticed something strange. The motor neurons of the monkey being studied were firing even though the monkey was not moving its limb. The monkey being studied was, however, watching another monkey move. As it turns out, viewing movement in another can fire the same neural network in the brain. This is now an area of compelling research and one of the applications happens to be pain processing.

Jackson, Meltzoff, and Decety (2005) explored empathy and pain. In this study, subjects observed photographs of potentially painful stimuli, such as getting a finger caught in a door, opening a door onto a toe, cutting a finger while slicing a vegetable, etc. The subjects were put in an fMRI scanner during the viewing of these pictures to detect what part of the brain activated while seeing another person in a potentially painful situation.

The researchers looked at two categories—the part of the brain that deals with the emotional aspect of pain (suffering) and also the physical representation of the area in the brain. The anterior cingulate cortex and the insula, two parts of the brain we have already shown to be very active in pain processing, lit up when watching another person in pain. These two parts of the brain are active with regard to the affective (emotional) component of pain processing. When watching the suffering of others, we also suffer.

Interestingly, the study did not see significant changes in the corresponding sensory area of the observer's brain. Viewing a photo of a toe about to be smashed by a door did not light up the sensory area in the viewer that would correspond to the toe. It did, however, light up the area that deals with the emotional aspect of the pain. One note, as made by the researchers, was that viewing a photograph of a toe about to be stubbed is not as strong a stimulus as perhaps a movie where a toe is indeed physically smashed by a door (couldn't get volunteers for that one!).

In the exploration of pain and the suffering of others, we have all experienced the variability of empathy in those around us. Some people have very little capability to experience pain empathy, that is, to experience the pain of others as painful to themselves. It could very well be that for whatever reason, some people have developed their empathetic capabilities more than others. Perhaps the science may also lead us to discover ways to develop that part of our brains, something that one would imagine to help us create a more humane and just world.

In the earlier explanation of the mechanism of empathy, it was dependent on the ability to draw on one's past experience to turn the pain of another into personal suffering. A deficit of personal experience is another way that loved ones and friends may not be able to empathize with the person in pain. In the previous research study, viewing a picture of a finger about to be sliced while cutting a vegetable resonates as a familiar experience for any of us who have wielded a kitchen knife. However, the pain of fibromyalgia or phantom limb pain is not likely to be a condition those around us have experienced, and thus can be empathetic to. The inability of friends, and especially family, to empathize with the person in pain can be seriously damaging to all concerned. The family and friends of the person in pain must learn to be careful and attentive listeners. Part of the purpose of this book is to help them understand the science of pain so that the second mechanism, that of extrapolated empathy (empathy not based on personal experience but on the ability to put oneself in the place of the other), can be encouraged.

A common impediment to being able to put oneself in the place of the pain sufferer is to falsely assess his/her present condition based on one's own experience. As we have learned, chronic pain and acute pain are two wildly different conditions. If one's only experience is with acute pain, pain that had a clear beginning and a clear timeline to recovery, it is tempting to wish the chronic pain sufferer would just suck it up and move forward. Understanding more deeply the mystery of pain should help the family and friends of the person in pain to be more empathetic and thus more supportive.

Pain and isolation

When I have interviewed people who suffer chronic pain, the overwhelming response I hear from them is that pain can be very isolating. One study, done by a website called "Pain Story" (www.painstory.org) found that 44 percent of pain sufferers felt alone in dealing with their pain. This matches my experience with people in pain. The responses of pain sufferers vary a bit, but there are definitely common themes. Many, if not most, are very reluctant to discuss their pain with friends and family. This is not hard to understand, for at least two reasons. One, the person in pain feels embarrassed to relay the unfortunate news that the pain isn't any better today than it was yesterday. In chronic pain, there may never be a resolution. For some pain sufferers, relaying the unchanging (and therefore negative) status feels like admitting failure day after day, especially if the people around them have never experienced chronic pain. For many in pain, saying nothing seems preferable. The downside of this strategy is that family members often have no idea how much suffering the person is really experiencing.

Another reason to withhold sharing the depth of the pain is that the sufferer really does not feel that the family is truly supportive. Fearing invalidation from the people you love is a devastating experience. As one woman told me, "I wish I had some sort of visible deformity or wound, so that people could see that my pain is real." Who can blame these people for not inviting ridicule? Compounding this, however, there is some evidence that people in chronic pain are overly sensitive about the depth of their significant other's relationship commitment.

This could create a situation where the loved one of someone in chronic pain feels undue pressure, that nothing the loved one can say or do will convince the pain sufferer of his/her support. What a delicate situation this becomes, and how fraught with irony. Clear and honest communication between the chronic pain sufferer and their loved ones is absolutely necessary, for the health of all concerned. If this is difficult for you with your immediate family, seeking professional guidance could be invaluable.

To address chronic pain through social support, numerous healthcare organizations have formed support groups for any number of pain conditions. The people who frequent these groups often find them extremely helpful for the power of shared experience. When I have suggested such a group to a chronic pain sufferer I think may be isolated, he/she often questions the value of a gathering. Most often, I hear the pain sufferer state that the group is not going to provide real solutions to the pain. While this is understandable, most attendees I have interviewed at these groups really appreciate the company of people who can understand their plight. Just being heard and accepted is enough to make attendance worthwhile. As with any group of this sort, that connection isn't going to happen with one miraculous visit. Trust is not an event: it is a process developed over time. The results of such an endeavor could have both immediate psychological benefit and perhaps far-reaching results too. Beginning with a landmark study (Spiegel *et al.* 1989), researchers have found numerous health benefits to these support groups. If one is available to you, consider joining.

For many pain sufferers, the advent of social networking via the internet has proved to be extremely helpful in creating community with others who really can understand the devastating reality of chronic pain. No longer bounded by time or geography, people who suffer from similar conditions can connect with peers across the globe. There are networks centered on a vast number of conditions, with people sharing current research, helpful tips for pain management, and also emotional support. Best of all, while there is the possibility for substantive emotional connection, there is also a certain level of anonymity in the online process. If you are a chronic pain sufferer, exploring online social support may indeed be very helpful and worth your time and energy. Whatever medium you choose, find a way to connect with others who can understand your plight.

CHAPTER **14**

THE PENDULUM
Now we know what causes <fill in the blank>

The longer I am in the field of healthcare, the more I have seen how the pendulum of understanding swings wildly. One might think that healthcare decisions are driven by reason and science, but this is often not the case because such decisions are made by people. Thus, healthcare decisions are driven by the same impulses that drive any other aspect of choice, not much of which is completely rational. There is no reason to think that healthcare would be different from other disciplines, except that the consequences of poor decisions could have dire consequences.

There is wisdom in being cautious in our healthcare decisions, not moving too quickly when new research or discoveries are unveiled. The shadow side of cautiousness is a seeming immobility and stasis; implementation of new ideas seems to take forever. In the end, moving cautiously is slightly preferable to a wild change of direction that proves incorrect at a later date. Every time the pendulum swings, innocent people in the path of the shift in understanding suffer. Here are several examples.

Pathogens and health

Louis Pasteur and Claude Bernard were giants in the field of medicine in the 1800s. Pasteur gave us valuable insight into the role of pathogens in the disease process. Bernard made a different case: these pathogens must have the right environment in which to prosper (which he called the milieu interieur). Without the right environment, the pathogen could not flourish. Pathogen or milieu—which is most important?

In reality, the answer is probably both. Unfortunately, the divisive debate continues to this day with passionate and knowledgeable people arguing for either extreme. For example, a very common perception is that the best way to protect against disease is to eat healthily, exercise, and get the correct amount of sleep. This seems quite reasonable and obvious at first glance; except that having a strong immune system is not always protective. Consider the influenza epidemic of 1918, where the flu was most deadly for those with the healthiest immune systems. What killed people was the immune system's vehement reaction to the virus, not the virus itself. The very young and the old simply got the flu, while the healthiest of the population died. Score one for Louis Pasteur.

Helicobacter bacteria and its role in ulcers is a fine example of pathogen and environment and their complex interaction. When Barry Marshall and J. Robin Warren first suggested that duodenal ulcers might be caused by the bacteria helicobacter, no one would listen to them. The prevailing wisdom was that ulcers cause stress, not bacteria. Exasperated that no one would listen, Marshall drank a whole Petri dish of helicobacter pylori and gave himself a raging ulcer in short order. Over time, it was shown that Marshall and Warren were correct: helicobacter can be an important factor in ulcers.

Instead of absorbing new information about the role of helicobacter pylori into what was already known and observed, the pendulum swung completely to the other side. (Stress has nothing to do with ulcers, ulcers are caused by bacteria. Score a point for Pasteur. But wait, don't mark that scorecard just yet...) Rather quickly, it became difficult to convince anyone that stress plays a role in ulcers. As Robert Sapolsky points out in his book

Why Zebras Don't Get Ulcers (1994), about 15 percent of the people with ulcers don't even have helicobacter. Worse yet, for every one hundred people infected with helicobacter, only ten will develop an ulcer. Why is that? If the bacteria cause ulcers, why doesn't everyone with helicobacter have an ulcer?

A new understanding, researched by Martin Blaser (Ackerman 2012), is that helicobacter pylori actually helps regulate the production of stomach acids. If there is too much acid, helicobacter pylori will produce a protein that slows down the production of acid production. Unfortunately, in some people, that protein (cagA) produces ulcers. To make matters even more interesting, helicobacter pylori has a possibly even more important side-effect. A hormone called ghrelin produced in the stomach tells the brain that we are hungry and need food. Interestingly, helicobacter pylori seems to regulate ghrelin. When helicobacter is eliminated (such as through antibiotics), ghrelin production is unchecked, and the hormone is produced even after consuming a full meal; thus the person is full and yet still hungry.

So it seems that the pathogen is important, but the complex relationships of the pathogen to its environment can produce both positive and negative outcomes. (Score one for Claude Bernard.)

Running shoe pendulum: Ultra-supportive vs. barefoot

For years, the running shoe industry has been producing ultra-cushioned shoes form-fitted to our individual foot structure. This effort was purported to provide the runner with a shoe tailored to his/her exact needs, correcting any perceived dysfunction. Using these high-end shoes was supposed to be protective against overuse injuries. Unfortunately, the resulting data isn't very positive: foot problems have generally increased over this period of time rather than decreased. As a result, the pendulum swings in exactly the opposite direction—the hot new trend is to run barefoot, shunning shoes completely.

At the heart of this debate is a very important principle, the continuum between support and challenge. As an example, if you give a vineyard all the moisture and nutrients it could want, the result will most likely be a very unimpressive wine. Vines that are stressed produce wine with great character. So it often is with people. People who get everything they want are generally pretty difficult to be around. Stress builds character.

With regard to feet, the muscles of the foot must be stressed and challenged to function and develop optimally. A perfect environment inside a shoe isn't going to do that. The opposite strategy is to remove all support, letting the foot respond to uneven surfaces and subtle balance changes. This would seem to be helpful in developing the intrinsic musculature of the foot.

Unfortunately, switching from cushy shoes to no shoe at all while running on concrete seems to be a very drastic change. Not surprisingly, foot specialists have seen a sharp increase in injuries as a result of the barefoot movement. While runners in Kenya do indeed run barefoot without injury, they have been barefoot from the moment they first walked. Plus, there is little resemblance between the savannah and a concrete sidewalk. My fear is that instead of applying the lessons of the support/ challenge continuum, the barefoot craze will soon be abandoned for the next new trend.

The pendulum and fibromyalgia

Fibromyalgia syndrome (FMS) is a perfect example of a swinging pendulum of understanding. In FMS, there is no clinically available definitive imaging technology that can reveal the pathology that causes FMS. In contrast, when a tumor is clearly seen on a diagnostic image, the surgeon's job is to skillfully remove the offending pathology. As a result, the accompanying pain disappears. What pathology can be removed by the doctor who specializes in the treatment of chronic pain?

This is an insight into why we as a society value (in money and esteem) the surgeon more than the physiatrist or rheumatologist (and probably the reason why these specialties are under-represented in medicine). The biomedical model is very strong in our culture, driven even deeper into our psyche by the increase in technology. Use the technology to observe the hidden pathology, attack and remove the source, and the patient's pain is now alleviated. In that very simple formula is the essence of the biomedical model. The assumptions are:

1. The cause can be seen.

2. Treatment can be directed to remove the source.

3. The pain is a result of the cause. Remove the cause and the pain disappears.

It should be abundantly clear that this process often does not apply to the treatment of pain. Pain cannot be seen on a screen. Often, no heroic procedure can remove the source. Quite often, pain is not just the reflection of a greater problem—in chronic pain, pain itself *is* the problem.

In a perfect storm of circumstances, along comes a syndrome that has no observable pathology, no clear answer, co-existing emotional and cognitive issues, and is predominately female. The setup for invalidation is massive; exactly what you will hear when speaking with women who have FMS. Their stories are painful to listen to. Many women have been told that FMS is merely an expression of "female problems." Most have been referred to psychological services, not as a way of coping with the pain, but under the assumption that deep-seated emotional conflict is the source of the pain. ("You feel bad and it is your fault.") These are very sad stories and often crushing experiences for FMS sufferers.

After years of doubt and invalidation from both physician and family, imagine the delight of FMS sufferers when a diagnosis and an actual name for their condition was announced. As you can imagine, thousands of FMS patients felt like saying, "I told you so." Many FMS sufferers speak powerfully about the experience of getting a name for the condition that has affected their life so negatively. There is a belief system within the biomedical model that a disease does not really exist until it has a name. Finally, these sufferers had a name for their malady, fibromyalgia.

Unfortunately, when the pendulum of medicine swings, people get hurt. It is a very common occurrence for physicians to see patients who have pain with no easily diagnosable cause. Unfortunately, there is no diagnostic code for "I don't know." Like everyone else, these patients with unexplained pain wanted a reason, a name, and therefore a context for the symptoms they experienced. Suddenly, there was a *possible* category to put these patients in: fibromyalgia. And get that diagnosis they did in droves. Unfortunately, over-diagnosing anyone with unexplained pain as having fibromyalgia caused the rest of the medical community to question the validity of fibromyalgia diagnosis en masse. This is perfectly understandable. If you understand the parameters of the diagnostic criteria and the majority of people diagnosed with FMS clearly do not meet that standard, one questions everything, including the very existence of the malady itself.

Unfortunately, the effect of questioning the validity of FMS had devastating effects on the original patients who have always had true FMS. They went from invalidated (no name for their malady), to validated (FMS diagnosis), to invalidated again (FMS isn't real, it is a garbage diagnosis) without doing anything. Almost worse, as so many physicians questioned the validity of FMS, this had a spillover effect on the lay public as well. The FMS diagnosis was rather synonymous with "they don't know what is wrong with you, so they gave it a name."

Friends, acquaintances, and even family still doubted the existence of FMS. What a frustrating rollercoaster ride: if one doctor definitively diagnoses you with FMS, imagine seeing another doctor later who asserts that FMS isn't a real problem. These aren't just casual acquaintances, these are doctors. In our culture, as in most, the opinion of a doctor about your health carries great weight. Even if you believe the doctor is incorrect, this encounter still has gravity and can create self-doubt that is not easy to dismiss.

The musculoskeletal pendulum

Another example of the swinging pendulum is in my own field of musculoskeletal pain. There are two competing models, defined clearly by the IASP (2010). One paradigm is represented by End Organ Dysfunction Model (EODM), the idea that there is something demonstrably wrong in the body. The other paradigm could be called an Altered Nervous System Processing Model (ANSPM). In this model, there is something wrong with the way the brain processes sensory information.

Proponents of the EODM point to clear pathologies in the body as the source of pain. A physician may point to a lumbar disc protruding into the spinal cord and causing pain down the leg. The chiropractor points to the altered structural position of a vertebra. A physical therapist may point to muscle imbalance and structural asymmetry. Proponents of the ANSPM will point to data showing that none of these conditions are reliable predictors of pain. If you follow subjects who present with structural asymmetry for several decades, you won't find them much more likely to have back pain than anyone else. Look at MRIs of people who have never had back pain and you will find the majority of them have serious disc pathology, but no pain.

The proponents of ANSPM make a very good point with regard to the data. On the other hand, we have years of clinical experience to show that there must be something to the EODM model. While some doubt the existence of trigger points, for instance, what do I tell the thousands of people I have helped over the years? Many thousands of people have had great success with chiropractic care—there must be something behind this. While we learned in earlier chapters that pain-free backs can have serious disc issues, countless back pain sufferers found disc surgery to be the *only* intervention that helped their constant back pain. Clearly, there must be a place for all of these approaches.

The same principle is probably true in the treatment of pain in general. As we have seen, there was a time when pain that was not understood by the doctor was perceived as an emotional problem of the patient. As diagnostic imaging became available, visible reasons for pain were discovered and the pendulum swung to treating the pathology being viewed. When this model showed deficiencies (observable pathology in non-symptomatic people), it happened to coincide with the emergence of a new understanding of the effect of our thoughts on biological processes. When this model was pushed too far (you are sick because of the way you think), the pendulum swung back to clearer and better imaging (MRI). Now, the ANSPM resurfaces with a movement away from finding a tangible source for pain in the body to how the brain perceives and processes information. The unintended shadow side of this model is that it is often perceived by the patient as invalidating. Patients understand this model to mean that the pain is less real if it is perceptual. In his/her mind, if it hurts this much the pain has to be "real," and "real" means that something is terribly wrong in the body.

Each time the pendulum of understanding swings due to advancement in understanding, the proponents of the new paradigm proclaim "now we know" what causes (fill in the blank with any disease or condition). Almost predictably, the coming decades will show that while there was some element of truth in this shift, it was not completely accurate. There were other factors not taken into consideration at the time, aspects of the condition that were poorly understood, or unintended consequences that followed. This is why, much to the consternation of many, science lurches forward a millimeter at a time. This deliberateness is necessary to protect against wild swings that later prove incorrect.

Moving forward

I share this debate with you in the hope that it will help you to evaluate the passionate voices that often occupy the extremes of any debate. There are bright people arguing both sides of the issue and these voices deserve to be heard. At the same time, it is important not to abandon the ideas of the past too quickly, especially if the results of treatments based on those ideas are at least respectable. Good science is like building a wall of knowledge, one brick at a time. It may be a slow process, but necessarily so if the wall is to stand the test of time.

That said, this book reflects the current understanding of pain which is bound to change over time. In addition, it is also reflected through the lens of my own understanding, which is also undergoing constant change. I hope I have reflected the science accurately, but I am sure the science, and my understanding of it, will undergo many additional changes in the next few years.

Even as the scientific understanding behind pain changes, one thing remains constant. Physicians and healthcare providers must listen carefully to their patients' experience of pain. Listening and observation are always powerful tools, especially when what we hear and observe does not fit into our current model of understanding. Being a healthcare provider who treats people in pain is often difficult and extremely humbling. Failure is commonplace; multiple strategies often must be explored before finding the most effective treatment methodology. Failure is an effective teacher, however, sharpening our skills and leading us to new ground if we admit our lack of understanding. As stated in the beginning of this book, mysteries exist because we do not understand the meaning of what is presented to us. We don't always need more data, we need a deeper understanding.

Good providers listen and observe carefully, withhold initial judgment, and enlist the patient's involvement in the treatment possibilities. As a result, the patient feels heard and validated in the process. That alone is powerful medicine.

REFERENCES

Chapter 3
That Which Can Be Known, But Not Often Seen

Chambers, C.T., Craig, K.D. and Bennett, S.M. (2002) "The impact of maternal behavior on children's pain experiences: an experimental analysis." *Journal of Pediatric Psychology 27*, 3, 293–301.

Dick-Read, G. (2004) *Childbirth Without Fear: The Principles and Practice of Natural Childbirth*. London: Pinter and Martin.

Dufton, L.M., Konik, B., Colletti, R., Stanger, C. *et al.* (2008) "Effects of stress on pain threshold and tolerance in children with recurrent abdominal pain." *Pain 136*, 1, 38–43.

Edwards, R.R., Doleys, D.M., Fillingim, R.B. and Lowery, D. (2001) "Ethnic differences in pain tolerance: clinical implications in a chronic pain population." *Psychosomatic Medicine 63*, 2, 316–323.

Evans, S., Tsao, J. and Zeltzer, L.K. (2008) "Relationship of child perceptions of maternal pain to children's laboratory and nonlaboratory pain." *Pain Research and Management 13*, 3, 211–218.

Green, C.R., Anderson, K.O., Baker, T.A., Campbell, L.C. *et al.* (2003) "The unequal burden of pain: confronting racial and ethnic disparities in pain." *Pain Medicine 4*, 3, 277–294.

Levine, F.M. and De Simone, L.L. (1991) "The effects of experimenter gender on pain report in male and female subjects." *Pain 44*, 69–72.

Taylor, S.E., Klein, L.C., Lewis, B.P., Gruenewald, T.L., Gurung, R.A.R. and Updegraff, J.A. (2000) "Biobehavioral responses to stress in females: tend-and-befriend, not fight-or-flight." *Psychological Review 107*, 411–429.

Wall, P.D. (2000) *Pain: The Science of Suffering*. New York: Columbia University Press.

Wise, E., Price, D., Myers, C., Heft, M. and Robinson, M. (2002) "Gender role expectations of pain: relationship to experimental pain perception." *Pain 96*, 3, 335–342.

Chapter 5
When the System Goes Awry

Freeman, M.D., Nystrom, A. and Centeno, C. (2009) "Chronic whiplash and central sensitization; an evaluation of the role of a myofascial trigger points in pain modulation." *Journal of Brachial Plexus and Peripheral Nerve Injury 4*, 2.

Melzack, R. and Wall, P.D. (1965) "Pain mechanisms: A new theory." *Science 150*, 971-979.

Richmond, C.E., Bromley, L.M. and Woolf, C.J. (1993) "Preoperative morphine pre-empts postoperative pain." *The Lancet 342*, 8863, 73–75.

Wall, P.D. and Woolf, C.J. (1984) "Muscle but not cutaneous C-afferent input produces prolonged increases in the excitability of the flexion reflex in the rat." *The Journal of Physiology 356*, 443–458.

Woolf, C.J. (2011) "Central sensitization: implications for the diagnosis and treatment of pain." *Pain 152*, 3, S2–15.

Chapter 6
The Importance of Meaning and Context

Gilovitch, T. (1993) *How We Know What Isn't So*. New York: Free Press.

Juhan, D. (2003) *Job's Body: A Handbook for Bodywork*. (First published 1987.) Barrytown, NY: Station Hill Press.

Scaer, R. (2001) *The Body Bears the Burden*. Binghampton, NY: Haworth Press.

Chapter 7
Attention and Pain

Bantick, S., Wise, R., Ploghaus, A., Clare, S., Smith, S. and Tracey, I. (2002) "Imaging how attention modulates pain in humans using functional MRI." *Brain 125*, 2, 310–319.

Berns, G., Chappelow, J., Cekic, M., Zink, C., Pagnoni, G. and Martin-Skurski, M. (2006) "Defining the neural basis of dread." *Science 312*, 5774, 653.

Bichot, N.P., Rossi, A.F. and Desimone, R. (2005) "Parallel and serial neural mechanisms for visual search in macaque area V4." *Science 308*, 5721, 529–534.

Chabris, C. and Simons, D. (2010) *The Invisible Gorilla*. New York: Crown Archetype.

Fields, H. (2009) "The psychology of pain." *Scientific American Mind 46*.

Grant, J.A. and Rainville, P. (2009) "Pain sensitivity and analgesic effects of mindful states in Zen meditators: A cross-sectional study." *Psychosomatic Medicine 71*, 106–114.

Keltner, J., Furst, A., Fan, C., Redfern, R., Inglis, B. and Fields, H. (2006) "Isolating the modulatory effect of expectation on pain transmission: a functional magnetic resonance imaging study." *Journal of Neuroscience 26*, 16, 4437–4443.

Kolata, G. (2010) "How to push past the pain, as the champions do." *New York Times, 18*.

MacLean, P.D. (1990) *The triune brain in evolution: Role in paleocerebral functions*. New York: Plenum Press.

Recanzone, G.H., Schreiner, C.E. and Merzenich, M.M. (1993) "Plasticity in the frequency representation of primary auditory cortex following discrimination training in adult owl monkeys." *The Journal of Neuroscience 13*, 1, 87–103.

Ogden, P., Minton, K. and Pain, C. (2006) *Trauma and the Body: A Sensorimotor Approach to Psychotherapy*. New York: Norton.

Sawamoto, N., Honda, M., Okada, T., Hanakawa, T. *et al.* (2000) "Expectation of pain enhances responses to nonpainful somatosensory stimulation in the anterior cingulate cortex and parietal operculum/posterior insula: an event-related functional magnetic resonance imaging study." *Journal of Neuroscience 20*, 19, 7438–7445.

Schwartz, J. and Begley, S. (2002) *The Mind and The Brain*. New York: Regan Books.

Chapter 8
Fear and Pain

Akerman, B. (2006) "When memory lane takes a wrong turn: Alleviating PTSD." *McGill Reporter 38*.

Bourne, P.G., Rose, R.M. and Mason, J.W. (1968) "17-OHCS levels in combat. Special forces 'A' team under threat of attack." *Archives of General Psychiatry 19*, 135–140.

Chou, R., Fu, R., Carrino, J. and Deyo, R. (2009) "Imaging strategies for low-back pain: systematic review and meta-analysis." *The Lancet 373*, 9662, 463–472.

Deyo, R.A., Diehl, A.K. and Rosenthal, M. (1986) "How many days of *bed rest* for acute low *back pain?*" *New England Journal of Medicine 315*, 1064–1070.

Depue, B.E., Curran, T. and Banich, M.T. (2007) "Prefrontal regions orchestrate suppression of emotional memories via a two-phase process." *Science 317*, 5835, 215–219.

Dolcos, F., LaBar, K. and Cabeza, R. (2005) "Emotional memories function in self-reinforcing loop." *ScienceDaily*. Available at www.sciencedaily.com/releases/2005/03/050323130625.htm, accessed on 19 November 2012.

Hodges, P. and Tucker, K. (2011) "Moving differently in pain: a new theory to explain the adaptation to pain." *Pain 152*, S90–S98.

Jensen, M., Brant-Zawadzki, M., Obuchowski, N., Modic, M., Malkasian, D. and Ross, J. (1994) "Magnetic resonance imaging of the lumbar spine in people without back pain." *New England Journal of Medicine 331*, 2, 69–73.

Laine, C., Goldman, D. and Wilson, J. (2008) "Low back pain." *Annals of Internal Medicine 148*, 9.

Lawndy, S., Withagen, M., Kluivers, K. and Vierhout, M. (2011) "Between hope and fear: patient's expectations prior to pelvic organ prolapse surgery." *International Urogynecology Journal 22*, 1159–1163.

Levine, P. (1997) *Waking the Tiger*. Berkeley, CA: North Atlantic Books.

Malmivaara, A., Häkkinen, U., Aro, T., Heinrichs, T. *et al.* "The treatment of acute low back pain: bed rest, exercises, or ordinary activity?" *New England Journal of Medicine 332*, 351–355.

Masui, T., Yukawa, Y., Nakamura, S., Kajino, G., Matsubara, Y., Kshiguro, N. *et al.* (2005) "Natural history of patients with lumbar disc herniation observed by magnetic resonance imaging for minimum 7 years." *Journal of Spinal Disorders and Techniques 18*, 2, 121–126.

McGill, S. (2002) *Low Back Disorders: Evidence Based Prevention and Rehabilitation*. Champaign, IL: Human Kinetics Publishers.

Mixter, W.J. and Barr, J.S. (1934) "Rupture of the intervertebral *disc* with involvement of the spinal canal." *New England Journal of Medicine 211*, 210–215.

Nader, K. and Einarsson, E. (2010) "Memory reconsolidation: an update." *Annals of the New York Academy of Sciences, 1191*, 27–41.

Ogden, P., Minton, K. and Pain, C. (2006) *Trauma and the Body: A Sensorimotor Approach to Psychotherapy.* New York: W. W. Norton & Company.

Payne, K.B. and Corrigan, E. (2007) "Emotional constraints on intentional forgetting." *Journal of Experimental Social Psychology 43*, 780–786.

Robinson, G.E. and Dyer, F.C. (1993) "Plasticity of spatial memory in honey bees: reorientation following colony fission." *Animal Behaviour 46*, 311–320.

Rothbaum, B., Hodges, L.F., Ready, D., Graap, K. and Alarcon, R.D. (2001) "Virtual reality exposure therapy for Vietnam veterans with posttraumatic stress disorder." *Journal of Clinical Psychiatry 62*, 8, 617-622.

Sapolsky, R. (2004) *Why Zebras Don't Get Ulcers.* New York: Henry Holt and Co.

Scaer, R. (2001) *The Body Bears the Burden: Trauma, Dissociation, and Disease.* New York: Haworth Medical Press.

Sime, A. M. (1976) "Relationship of preoperative fear, type of coping, and information received about surgery to recovery from surgery." *Journal of Personality and Social Psychology 34*, 4, 716–724.

University of Queensland (2008) "New understanding of how we remember traumatic events." *ScienceDaily.* Available at www.sciencedaily.com/releases/2008/10/081028103111.htm, accessed on 19 November 2012.

Weinstein, J.N., Tosteson, T.D., Lurie, J.D., Tosteson, A.N.A. *et al.* (2006) "Surgical vs. nonoperative treatment for lumbar disk herniation. The spine patient outcomes research trial (SPORT): a randomized trial." *Journal of the American Medical Association 296*, 20, 2441–2450.

Chapter 9
Placebos and the Placebo Effect

Goebel, M.U., Meykadeh, N., Kou, W., Schedlowski, M. and Hengge, U.R. (2008) "Behavioral conditioning of antihistamine effects in patients with allergic rhinitis." *Psychotherapy and Psychosomatics 77*, 227–234.

Kaptchuk, T.J., Friedlander, E., Kelley, J.M., Sanchez, M.N. *et al.* (2010) "Placebos without deception: a randomized controlled trial in irritable bowel syndrome." *PLoS ONE 5*, 12, e15591.

McRae, C., Cherin, E., Yamazaki, T.G., Diem, G. *et al.* (2004) "Effects of perceived treatment on quality of life and medical outcomes in a double-blind placebo surgery trial." *Archives of General Psychiatry 61*, 4, 412–420.

Moseley, J.B., O'Malley, K., Petersen, N.J., Menke, T.J. *et al.* (2002) "A controlled trial of arthroscopic surgery for osteoarthritis of the knee." *New England Journal of Medicine 347*, 81–88.

Olds, J. and Milner, P. (1954) "Positive reinforcement produced by electrical stimulation of septal area and other regions of rat brain." *Journal of Comparative and Physiological Psychology, 47*, 419–427.

Pacheco-López, G., Riether, C., Doenlen, R., Engler, H. *et al.* (2009) "Calcineurin inhibition in splenocytes induced by pavlovian conditioning." *FASEB Journal 23*, 4, 1161–1167.

Shiv, B., Carmon, Z. and Ariely, D. (2005) "Placebo effects of marketing actions: consumers may get what they pay for."*Journal of Marketing Research XLII* , 383–393.

Waber, R.L., Shiv, B., Carmon, Z. and Ariely, D. (2008) "Commercial features of placebo and therapeutic efficacy." *Journal of the American Medical Association 299*, 9, 1016–1017.

Chapter 10
Phantom Limb Pain

Giraux, P. and Sirigu, A. (2003) "Illusory movements of the paralyzed limb restore motor cortex activity." *NeuroImage 20*, S107–S111.

Ramachandran, V.S. and Blakeslee, S. (1998) *Phantoms in the Brain: Probing the Mysteries of the Human Mind.* New York: William Morrow.

Chapter 11
Trigger Points and Referred Pain

Travell, J.G. and Simons, D.G. (1992) *Myofascial Pain and Dysfunction: The Trigger Point Manual* (vol 2). Baltimore, MD: Williams and Wilkins.

Chapter 12
Fibromyalgia

American Pain Society (2008) "Fibromyalgia pain linked with central nervous system disorder." *Science Daily.* Availble at: www.sciencedaily.com/releases/2008/05/080531091216.htm, accessed on 27 May 2009.

Buskila, D., Neumann, L., Vaisberg, G., Alkalay, D. and Wolfe, F. (1997) "Increased rates of fibromyalgia following cervical spine injury." *Arthritis Rheumatism 40*, 446–452.

Chang, L., Mayer, E.A., FitzGerald, L., Stains, J. and Naliboff, B. (2000) "Differences in somatic perception in patients with irritable bowel syndrome with and without fibromyalgia." *Pain 84*, 2–3, 297–307.

Guedj, E., Cammilleri, S., Niboyet, J., Dupont, P. *et al.* (2008) "Clinical correlate of brain SPECT perfusion abnormalities in fibromyalgia." *Journal of Nuclear Medicine*, November 2008; DOI: 10.2967/jnumed.108.053264.

Harris, R., Clauw, D., Scott, D., McLean, S., Gracely, R. and Zubieta, J.K. (2007) "Decreased central μ-opioid receptor availability in fibromyalgia." *Journal of Neuroscience 27*, 37, 10000–10006.

Leavitt, F. and Katz, R. (2012) "Lexical memory deficit in fibromyalgia syndrome." *Journal of Musculoskeletal Pain 20*, 2, 82–86.

Moldofsky, H. (2002) "Management of sleep disorders in fibromyalgia." *Rheumatic Disease Clinics of North America 28*, 2, 353–365.

Staud, R. (2006) "Biology and therapy of fibromyalgia: pain in fibromyalgia syndrome." *Arthritis Research and Therapy 8*, 3, 208.

Wolfe, F., Smythe, H.A., Yunus, M.B., Bennett, R.M., *et al.* (1990) "The American College of Rheumatology 1990 criteria for the classification of fibromyalgia. Report of the Multicenter Criteria Committee." *Arthritis and Rheumatism 33*, 2, 160–172.

Chapter 13
Social Support and Pain

di Pellegrino, G., Fadiga, L., Fogassi, L., Gallese, V. and Rizzolatti, G. (1992) "Understanding motor events: a neurophysiological study." *Experimental Brain Research 91*, 1, 176–180.

Eisenberger, N.I. and Lieberman, M.D. (2004) "Why rejection hurts: a common neural alarm system for physical and social pain." *Trends in Cognitive Sciences 8*, 294–300.

Eisenberger, N.I., Jarcho, J.M., Lieberman, M.D. and Naliboff, B. (2006) "An experimental study of shared sensitivity to physical pain and social rejection." *Pain 126*, 132–138.

Gallese, V., Fadiga, L., Fogassi, L. and Rizzolatti, G. (1996) "Action recognition in the premotor cortex." *Brain 119*, 2, 593–609.

Jackson, P.L., Meltzoff, A.N. and Decety, J. (2005) "How do we perceive the pain of others? A window into the neural processes involved in empathy." *Neuroimage 24*, 3, 771–779.

Master, S.L., Eisenberger, N.I., Taylor, S.E., Naliboff, B.D., Shirinyan, D. and Lieberman, M.D. (2009) "A picture's worth: partner photographs reduce experimentally induced pain." *Psychological Science 20*, 1316–1318.

Spiegel, D., Bloom, J.R., Kraemer, H.C. and Gottheil, E. (1989) "Effects of psychological treatment on survival of patients with metastatic breast cancer." *The Lancet ii*, 888–891.

Younger, J., Aron, A., Parke, S., Chatterjee, N. and Mackey, S. (2010) "Viewing pictures of a romantic partner reduces experimental pain: involvement of neural reward systems." *PLoS ONE 5*, 10, e13309. doi 10.1371/journal.pone.0013309.

Chapter 14
The Pendulum

Ackerman, J. (2012) "The ultimate social network." *Scientific American 42*.

International Association for the Study of Pain (IASP) (2010) "Clinical updates *low back pain.*" *IASP Journal of Pain XVIII*, 6.

Sapolsky, R. (1994) *Why Zebras Don't Get Ulcers*. New York: Holt Paperbacks.

RECOMMENDED READING

Chapter 3
That Which Can Be Known, But Not Often Seen

Wickelgren, I. (2009) "I do not feel your pain." *Scientific American Mind*, 51–57.

Chapter 7
Attention and Pain

Duke University (2000) "New study identifies brain centers for attention control." *ScienceDaily*. Retrieved December 29, 2012, from www.sciencedaily.com/releases/2000/02/000224075505.htm

Hadjistavropoulos, H.D., Hadjistavropoulos, T. and Quine, A. (2000) "Health anxiety moderates the effects of distraction versus attention to pain." *Behaviour Research and Therapy 38*, 5, 425–438.

Lutz, A., Slagter, H.A., Dunne, J.D. and Davidson, R.J. (2008) "Attention regulation and monitoring in meditation." *Trends in Cognitive Sciences 12*, 4, 163–169.

Chapter 8
Fear and Pain

Asmundson, G.J.G., Wright, K.D. and Hadjistavropoulos, H.D. (2005) "Hypervigilance and attentional fixedness in chronic musculoskeletal pain: consistency of findings across modified stroop and dot-probe tasks." *The Journal of Pain, 6*, 497–506.

Cahill, L., Prins, B., Weber, M. and McGaugh, J. (1994) "β-Adrenergic activation and memory for emotional events." *Nature 371*, 702–704; DOI: 10.1038/371702a0.

Cook, A.J., Brawer, P. and Vowles, K. (2006) "The fear-avoidance model of chronic pain: validation and age analysis using structural equation modeling." *Pain 121*, 3, 195–206.

Crombez, G., Eccleston, C., Van Den Broeck, A., Van Houdenhove, B. and Goubert, L. (2002) "The effects of catastrophic thinking about pain on attentional interference by pain: no mediation of negative affectivity in healthy volunteers and in patients with low back pain." *Pain Research and Management 7*, 31–39.

Gerardi, M., Rothbaum, B., Ressler, K., Heekin, M. and Rizzo, A. (2008) "Virtual reality exposure therapy using a virtual Iraq: case report." *Journal of Traumatic Stress 21*, 2, 209–213.

Helmstetter, F. and Fanselow, M. (1993) "Aversively motivated changes in meal patterns of rats in a closed economy: the effects of shock density." *Learning and Behavior 21*, 2, 168–175.

Morris, R., Furlong, T. and Westbrook, R. (2005) "Recent exposure to a dangerous context impairs extinction and reinstates lost fear reactions." *Journal of Experimental Psychology: Animal Behaviour Processes 31*, 40–55.

Morris, R., Westbrook, F. and Killcross, A. (2005) "Reinstatement of extinguished fear by β-adrenergic arousal elicited by a conditioned context." *Behavioral Neuroscience 119*, 1662–1671.

Peters, M.L., Vlaeyen, J.W.S. and Weber, W.E.J. (2005) "The joint contribution of physical pathology, pain-related fear and catastrophizing to chronic back pain disability." *Pain 113*, 45–50.

Sacktor, T.C. and Mzeta, P.K. (2008) "LTP maintenance, and the dynamic molecular biology of memory storage." *Progress in Brain Research 169*, 27–40.

Sullivan, M.J.L., Lynch, M.E. and Clark, A.J. (2005) "Dimensions of catastrophic thinking associated with pain experience and disability in patients with neuropathic pain conditions." *Pain 113*, 310–315.

Turner, J.A., Mancl, L. and Aaron, L.A. (2004) "Pain-related catastrophizing: a daily process study." *Pain 110*,103–111.

Chapter 9
Placebos and the Placebo Effect

Goebel, M.U., Trebst, A.E., Steiner, J., Xie, Y.F. *et al.* (2002) "Behavioral conditioning of immunosuppression is possible in humans." *FASEB J. 16*, 14, 1869–1873.

Chapter 10
Phantom Limb Pain

Chahine, L. and Kanazi, G. (2007) "Phantom limb syndrome: a review." *Middle East Journal of Anesthesiology 19*, 2.

Flor, H. (2002) "Phantom-limb pain: characteristics, causes, and treatment." *The Lancet, Neurology 1*.

Flor, H., Denke, C., Schaefer, M. and Grüsser, S. (2001) "Effect of sensory discrimination training on cortical reorganisation and phantom limb pain." *The Lancet, 357*.

Furlan, A.D., Pennick, V., Bonbardier, C. and van Tulden, M. (2003) "Cortical reorganisation and chronic pain: implications for rehabilitation." *Journal of Rehabilitation Medicine, Suppl. 41*, 66–72.

215

Chapter 12
Fibromyalgia

Holman, A.J. (2008) "Positional cervical spinal cord compression and fibromyalgia: A novel comorbidity with important diagnostic and treatment implications." *The Journal of Pain 9*, 7, 613–622.

Staud, R. and Smitherman, M.L. (2002) "Peripheral and central sensitization in fibromyalgia: pathogenetic role." *Current Pain and Headache Reports 6*, 4, 259–266.

University of Michigan Health System (2007) "Why don't painkillers work for people with fibromyalgia?" *ScienceDaily 3*.

Chapter 13
Social Support and Pain

Ciechanowski, P., Sullivan, M., Jensen, M., Romano, J. and Summers, H. (2003) "The relationship of attachment style to depression, catastrophizing and health care utilization in patients with chronic pain." *Pain 104*, 627–637.

SUBJECT INDEX

Page references in *italic* indicate
Figures.

ACC *see* anterior cingulate cortex
acute pain 23–9
  and the antialgic position
    27–8
  and the Central Governor
    Theory 24–5
  and enforced rest 26
  and memory 27
  as a scorecard 26
  source identification and
    elimination 27
  as a teacher 26–7
addiction 142
afferent information 56
aging 71, 174
allodynia 52, 176
Altered Nervous System
  Processing Model
  (ANSPM) 204–5
amygdala 77–8, 90, 111–12,
  111, 113, 114–15, 178
  inter-relationship with
    hippocampus 77–8,
    113–14
  and the placebo effect
    141–2
ANSPM (Altered Nervous
  System Processing Model)
  204–5
anterior cingulate cortex (ACC)
  86–8, *87*, 178, 193
  dorsal (dACC) 188–90
antialgic position 27–8
anxiety 104
athletes' pain 17, 100
  and the Central Governor
    Theory 24–5
  and menstruation of young
    female gymnasts 39
  tolerance 37–8
attention
  and the brain 80–82, 84–5
  directed away from pain 95–
    101 *see also* distraction
  directed from the top down
    93–4

  and expectation 85–9, 101
  focused (meditation) 95
  linking with emotion 98
  and novelty 98
  and pain 80–102
  preselection 97
  reduction of pain through
    92–101
  selective 82–9, 97–101
  and signal strength 98
awareness 77, 95

baboons 187–8
back pain
  and the Altered Nervous
    System Processing
    Model 204
  and diagnostic imaging
    128–32
  and fear of movement
    120–22
  low back pain and bed rest
    121–2
  visceral problems presenting
    as 45, 46
  and walking speed 119–20
Balfour, William 157
barefoot running 201
bed rest, with lower back pain
  121–2
Beecher, Henry K. 136
bees 105–6
beliefs
  and the nocebo effect 137
  and the placebo effect 135–
    40, 142–5
Bernard, Claude 198, 199
biomedical model 202–3
bladder infection 46–7
bottom-up processing by the
  brain 93–4
brain
  amygdala *see* amygdala
  anterior cingulate cortex
    86–8, *87*, 178, 188–9,
    193
  areas which may play a role
    in pain *113*
  and attention 80–82, 84–5

best guess phenomenon
  118, 151
bottom-up processing 93–4
  and the Central Governor
    Theory 24–5
  and central sensitization 62,
    183–4
  and dispassion 95
  dorsal anterior cingulate
    cortex 188–90
  effects of expectation of pain
    86–9, 137
  effects of pain on centers and
    areas 32
  effects of thinking about pain
    89–92, 193
  efferent processing 59
  and empathy 193
  and fear 90, 111–12, *111,*
    115
  and fibromyalgia 182, 183
  hard-wired concept of
    149–50
  'high road' processing 111,
    111, 112, 117
  hippocampus *see*
    hippocampus
  imaging *87*, 88, 91, 96–7,
    99, 114, 124, 137,
    142, 183, 193
  limbic/mid-brain 81, 82,
    89, 93
  locus coeruleus 182
  'low road' processing 111–
    12, *111*
  modulation of pain 57–9
  and movement 120–21
  neocortex 81–2, 89, 93
  neural plasticity 98–100,
    149–50
  nucleus accumbens 142,
    178, 191–2
  parietal operculum 86
  Penfield homunculus 148–9,
    149
  and the perceived meaning of
    stimuli 64–79
  and phantom limb pain
    148–53

brain *cont.*
   and the placebo effect
      141–2
   posterior insula 86
   remapping 149–50
   reptilian 81
   right ventral prefrontal cortex
      190
   rounding up/best guess 118,
      120, 151
   and social distress 188–90
   spillover effect 190
   stem 182
   top-down processing 93,
      112
   trigeminal nucleus caudalis
      182
   triune model 81

C fibres 48, 49–50, 51, 55
cagA protein 200
Cahill, Larry 115
Cajal, Santiago Ramon y
      149–50
cancer 144
   stomach 45
catastrophizing 119–20
Central Governor Theory 24–5
central nervous system (CNS)
      51, 52–3
central sensitization 60–64,
      60, 119, 183–4,
      185–6
   and fibromyalgia 183–4,
      184, 185–6
cervical spine injury/whiplash
      77, 181–182
chemical nociceptors 44
childbirth 40–41
chronic pain 29–32
   and the C fiber network 48,
      49–50, 55
   complexity of 29–30
   evolutionary use of 31–2
   of fibromyalgia *see*
      fibromyalgia syndrome
      (FMS)
   IASP definition 29
   mechanisms 32
   and memory 104–17
   models of 13
   non-linear 13
   sensitization to *see*
      sensitization to pain
   source location 49
CIP (Congenital Indifference to
      Pain) 28–9, 47
CNS *see* central nervous system
cognition 81–2
   loss, with fibromyalgia 181
   pain and thinking about pain
      89–92

comfort-seeking, the antialgic
      position 27–8
conditioning 73, 101, 107, 141
   fear 104, 115
   in placebo effect 136,
      140–42
Congenital Indifference to Pain
      (CIP) 28–9, 47
context of stimuli 65–79
control, sense of 131, 132–4
cortisol 133–4
Counting Stroop Test 96–7
culture, and pain tolerance
      40–41

dACC (dorsal anterior cingulate
      cortex) 188–90
Darvocet 178
defensive behavior system
      103–4
   see also fear
A delta fibres 48–9, 51–2
depression 178, 182
Descartes, René 23
diagnosis of pain 15–16
   denial/questioning of the
      reality of patient's
      experience of pain 21,
      70, 147, 178, 202–4
   diagnostic imaging and
      reality 127–32
   and fear 126–32
   and the language of internal
      organ pain 45–7
   and self-doubt 21, 70
dispassion 95
distraction 58, 95–101, 191–2
   see also pre-synaptic inhibition
dopamine 142
dorsal anterior cingulate cortex
      (dACC) 188–90
dorsal horn 56
dread 90–92
duodenal ulcers 199–200

efferent processing 59
emotions
   and the amygdala 77, 90,
      111–12, 113–15
   control of emotional
      reactivity through the
      brain 117
   effects of pain on emotional
      centers of the brain 32
   emotional components of
      a painful memory
      110–16
   emotional experience as a
      factor of pain 19–20,
      110–11, 112–13, 136
      see also psychological
      pain

fear *see* fear
   with visual images 112–13
empathy 192–5
End Organ Dysfunction Model
      (EODM) 204–5
endorphins 101
EODM (End Organ Dysfunction
      Model) 204–5
estrogen 39
expectation, and pain
   effects on the brain 86–9,
      137
   gender role expectations
      38–9
   negative 85–9
   positive 101
expectation, conditioning
      through *see* conditioning

Faces Scale of pain *35*
fatigue, with fibromyalgia 179
fear
   and anxiety 104
   and the brain 90, 111–12,
      111, 115
   conditioning 104, 115
   and diagnosis 126–32
   of irreversible consequences
      130
   leading to hyper-vigilance
      and catastrophizing
      118–20
   and memory 105–17
   of movement (kinesiophobia)
      120–26
   and pain 103–34
   as a primal system of
      defensive behaviors
      103
   prompting questioning and
      understanding 134
   responses 111–12, *111*
   and sense of control 132–4
   suspension of 111
fibromyalgia syndrome (FMS)
      52, 175–86, 201–4
   and the blurred lines of
      symptom causation
      185–6, 201–4
   and the brain 182, 183
   diagnosis 175–6, 201–4
   and fatigue 179
   formal recognition and
      classification 175–6
   and gender 178, 202
   and IBS 180–81
   and loss of cognition 181
   and migraine 181–3
   post-exercise soreness 179
   and sleep disorders 179–80
   and the technological culture
      201–4

tender point examination
176–7, *177*
treatment 178–9
wind-up and temporal
summation with
184–5
fight, flight, freeze model 59
fight or flight mechanism 123
fMRI *see* functional magnetic
resonance imaging
FMS *see* fibromyalgia syndrome
Focused Attention 95
footwear, running shoes
200–201
freezing/freeze mode 122–4
functional magnetic resonance
imaging (fMRI) *87*, 88,
91, 96–7, 99, 114, 124,
137, 142, 193

gall bladder 45
gate control theory of pain 59
gender
bias in treatment of pain 178
FMS denigration as
expression of female
problems 202
and pain threshold 38
and pain tolerance 38–9
role expectations of pain
38–9
ghrelin 200
Gladwell, Malcolm 13
globulin 55–6

Hackett, George 169–70
happiness 188
headaches 168–9
heart 45–6
helicobacter bacteria 199–200
Helleday, Uno 157
hippocampus 78, *113*, 118
inter-relationship with
amygdala 77–8,
113–14
and the placebo effect 141,
142
histamine 55–6
hyper-vigilance 118–20
hypersensitivity 51, 52–4, 55,
60–63
to cold 182
hyperalgesia with FMS 180
to sound 182
and the twitch response
160–61
hypnosis 102
hypoalgesia 180

IASP *see* International
Association for the Study
of Pain
IBS *see* Irritable Bowel Syndrome
imagery, positive 101–2
infection, and chronic pain
31–2, 46–7
International Association for the
Study of Pain (IASP) 190
definition of pain 18–20,
29, 103, 110
models of musculoskeletal
pain 204–5
Irritable Bowel Syndrome (IBS)
and fibromyalgia 180–81
migraines with 182
and the placebo effect 143
isolation 195–7
itching 59

Job, suffering of 66–7
joint nociceptors 44–5
jump sign 160–61

Kellgren, John 157–8
Kennedy, John F. 156–7
kidney 45
kinesiophobia 120–26

Laesch, Walter 41
Leao, Aristides 182
LeDoux, Joseph 103, *111*
life expectancy 188
limbic system 81
see also mid-brain
locus coeruleus 182
love 190–92
low back pain (LBP) 120–22
and diagnostic imaging
128–32

Macaque monkey 193
magnetic resonance imaging
(MRI) 15, 93, 127–32,
205
functional *see* functional
magnetic resonance
imaging (fMRI)
Marshall, Barry 199
meaning, and pain 65–79
measurement of pain
Faces Scale *35*
patient reporting difficulties
35–41
reframing the scale 41
threshold 36–7, 38–9
tolerance 37, 38–9
Verbal Reporting Scale 34,
34, 35
Visual Analog Scale 34–5,
35, 38

mechanosensitive nociceptors
44, 45
medication 63–4, 132–3, 136,
141, 178
meditation 95
Mediterranean diet 188
memory
accuracy, fragility and
implications in pain
108–16
and acute pain 27
blocking formation 116
and chronic pain 104–17
consolidation 116
and the control of emotional
reactivity 117
emotional components of
a painful memory
110–16
fibromyalgia and difficulties
with 181
formation 112, 116
using its plasticity to decrease
pain 117
pharmacological agents to
influence traumatic
memories 115–16
reconsolidation 109–10
and the rounding up of the
brain 118
Merzenich, Michael 149, 150,
158
*see also his entry in the author
index*
Mexger, Johan 157
mid-brain 81, 82, 89, 93
migraines 168–9
and fibromyalgia 181–3
and IBS 182
milieu 199
mirror box 151–2
mirror neurons 193
Mitchell, Silas Weir 147
models of pain *see* pain models
modulation of pain 57–9
morphine 63, 178
motor inhibition 164–5
motor neurons 193
movement
and back pain 119–22
and the brain 120–21
fear of (kinesiophobia)
120–26
after a freeze 123, 124
as inhibitor of pain 125–6
and muscular action 120–21
MRI *see* magnetic resonance
imaging
muscle overload 172–3
muscular action 120–21
muscular weakness 164–5, 174

musculoskeletal pain 155–7,
204–6
fibromyalgia see fibromyalgia
syndrome (FMS)
models 204–5
pain-spasm-pain cycle
concept 163–4
referred see referred pain/
sensation
trigger points see trigger
points, myofascial
Myofascial Pain Syndrome 176
myofascial trigger points see
trigger points, myofascial

NAcc (nucleus accumbens) 142,
178, 191–2
National Institute for Mental
Health 150
neocortex/Neomammalian brain
81–2, 89, 93
nerve root compression 173
nervous system 14–15, 23
A delta fibres 48–9, 51–2
and afferent information 56
Altered Nervous System
Processing Model
204–5
C fibres 48, 49–50, 51, 55
central see central nervous
system (CNS)
conditioning see conditioning
efferent processing 59
fight, flight, freeze model 59
hyper-excitation 57, 182
and movement 120–21
neural inhibition 57–9
neural plasticity 98–100
nociceptors see nociceptors
repetition and wind-up
54–5, 185
sensitization see sensitization
to pain
sympathetic 181
neural inhibition 57–9
neural plasticity 98–100
neutrophils 31–2
Nielsen, Brenda 31
nocebo effect 137
nociceptors 43, 44–9
and allodynia 52
chemical 44
and chemical release 55–6
and CIP 47
detecting potential damage
47–8
and heightened sensitivity
51, 52–4, 55, 60–63
see also hypersensitivity
joint 44–5
mechanosensitive 44, 45
peripheral receptors 68

and peripheral sensitization
51–9, 119, 183–4
polymodal 44
silent 44–5, 46
thermal 44
visceral 45–7
noradrenaline/norepinephrine
112
nucleus accumbens (NAcc) 142,
178, 191–2

Open Presence 95
opioids 63, 178
Oxycontin 178

pain
acute see acute pain
and aging 71
allodynia 52
and associated phenomena
46–7
of athletes see athletes' pain
and attention see attention
back see back pain
and being understood
187–97
bilateral 183
and the brain see brain
C fibre 49–50, 51, 55
chronic see chronic pain
chronology and 74–5
Congenital Indifference to
28–9, 47
context and the perceived
meaning of stimuli
64–79
control see pain control/
reduction
definitions and nature 17–
22, 29, 103, 110 see
also pain models
diagnosing see diagnosis
of pain
and dread 90–92
and empathy 192–5
errant meanings/
presentations of
70–73
expectation of see expectation,
and pain
and fear see fear
fibromyalgia see fibromyalgia
syndrome (FMS)
and freezing 122–4
gate control theory of 59
and gender see gender
and isolation 195–7
language of internal organ
pain 45–7
as life-saving 23–9
measuring see measurement
of pain

mechanical 46
and memory see memory
modulation 57–9
musculoskeletal see
musculoskeletal pain
perception and 65–79
phantom limb 146–54
physiology of see nervous
system; nociceptors
post-exercise soreness 179
post-trauma experience
75–9
and predictability 73–4,
77, 79
psychological see
psychological pain
and randomness 74, 86–9
reduction see pain control/
reduction
referred see referred pain/
sensation
scales 34–5, 34, 35, 38, 41
sensitization to see
sensitization to pain
and social distress 188–90
and social support see social
support
and suffering 17–18, 19
suppression 39
and the technological culture
201–4
and thinking about pain
89–92
threshold of see pain
threshold
tolerance of see pain tolerance
trigger points see trigger
points, myofascial
visual components 112–13
volitional vs non-volitional
100–101
pain control/reduction
through attention 92–101
through distraction 58,
95–101, 191–2
and gate control theory 59
through hypnosis 102
through love 190–92
through medication 63–4,
132–3, 141, 178
through movement 125–6
through neural inhibition
57–9
through Patient Controlled
Analgesia 132–3
placebo effect see placebo
effect
using plasticity of memory
117
through positive expectation
101
through positive imagery
101–2

pain mechanisms
    chronic pain 32
    nociceptors *see* nociceptors
pain models 13–14
    acute pain 23–9
    Altered Nervous System
        Processing Model
        204–5
    biomedical 22, 202–3
    and the Central Governor
        Theory 24–5
    End Organ Dysfunction
        Model 204–5
    frustration resulting from old
        models 21–2
    musculoskeletal pain 204–5
    pain as a byproduct of
        pathology 22, 202–3
    pain as an exactor of justice
        18
    pain as perception 68–70
    pain as a punishment 17–18,
        67
    pain as a warning 13, 18,
        23–9, 146, 147
    and phantom limb pain 146,
        147
pain process
    and the amygdala 77–8,
        111–12, *111*, 113–14
    models *see* pain models
    multiple factors of 15
    sensitization *see* sensitization
        to pain
pain threshold 36–7
    chemicals lowering the
        threshold of sensitivity
        56
    and gender 38
    tests 36–7, 38–9
pain tolerance 36, 37–41
    and childbirth 40–41
    and culture 40–41
    and gender 38–9
    and meditation practice 95
    and stress 37
Paleomammalian brain 81, 82,
    89, 93
parietal operculum (PO) 86
Pasteur, Louis 198–9
pathogens 198–200
Patient Controlled Analgesia
    (PCA) 132–3
Pavlov, Ivan 73–4, 104, 105,
    140–41
PCA (Patient Controlled
    Analgesia) 132–3
Penfield, Wilder 148–9
Penfield homunculus 148–9,
    149
People for the Ethical Treatment
    of Animals (PETA) 150

perception, and pain 65–79
peripheral sensitization 51–9,
    119, 183–4
phantom limb pain 146–54
PI (posterior insula) 86
Pitman, Roger 115
PKMzeta enzyme 116
placebo effect 135–42
    in animals 140
    and belief 135–40, 142–5 .
    and the brain 141–2
    and conditioning of the
        nervous system 136,
        140–42
    and perceptions of cost
        137–8
    in surgery 139–40
polymodal nociceptors 44
Pons, Timothy 150
positive expectation 101
positive imagery, and pain
    reduction 101–2
post-exercise soreness, FMS
    178–9
post-synaptic inhibition 57–8
post-trauma experience 75–9
    Post-Traumatic Stress
        Disorder 105,
        115–16
posterior insula (PI) 86
potassium ions 55–6
pre-synaptic inhibition 58–9
predictability 73–4, 77, 79
progesterone 39
propranolol 115, 116
prostaglandins 55–6
protein kinases 55–6
psychological pain 17, 18
    emotional element of pain
        experience 19–20,
        110–11, 112–13, 136
        see also emotions
    pain (mis-)ascribed to
        psychological causes
        16, 21–2, 153, 178,
        202
PTSD (Post-Traumatic Stress
    Disorder) 105, 115–16
punishment 17–18, 67

Raglin, John S. 100–101
Ramachandran, Vilayanur S.
    148, 150–53
randomness 74, 86–9
referred pain/sensation 157–8,
    162–5
    ligaments and joints as
        possible sources
        169–71
    mechanism of 171–2
    mimicked symptoms 165–9
    patterns 170, *170*

trigger points *see* trigger
    points, myofascial
and weakness 164–5
replication of symptoms 161–2
reptilian brain 81
rest
    enforced 26
    with low back pain 121–2
right ventral prefrontal cortex
    (RVPFC) 190
running shoes 200–201
RVPFC (right ventral prefrontal
    cortex) 190

Sapolsky, Robert 187–8
    *see also his entry in the author
        index*
Sarno, John 124
self-prophecy 90
sensitization to pain 30–31,
    180–181
    central 60–64, *60*, 119,
        183–4, 185–6
    and chemical release 55–6
    heightened sensitivity *see*
        hypersensitivity
    hypoalgesia with IBS 180
    local sensitivity 186
    lowering the threshold of
        sensitivity 56
    neural inhibition 57–9
    peripheral 51–9, 119,
        183–4
    post-synaptic inhibition
        57–8
    pre-synaptic inhibition 58–9
    wind-up/summation with
        repetition 54–5, 185
sensorimotor psychotherapy 94
serotonin 55–6
Simons, Daniel 82–3
Simons, David 155, 159, 161
single photon emission
    computed tomography
    (SPECT) 183
sleep disorders
    with fibromyalgia 179–80
    and migraines 182
'Snowworld' 102
social distress 188–90
social support 187–97
    and empathy 192–5
    and the isolating effects of
        pain 195–7
SPECT (single photon emission
    computed tomography)
    183
spillover effect, cerebral 190
spinal cord 56
    cervical spine injury/
        whiplash 77,
        182–183

spleen 45
Staub, William 173
sternocleidomastoid muscle
    168–9
stomach cancer 45
Strauss, Dr 157
stress
    effect of social networks on
        187–8
    and IBS 180–81
    and pain tolerance 37
    positive 201
    PTSD 105, 115–16
    responses 107–8, 133
    and the sense of control
        133–4
    social distress 188–90
    and ulcers 199–200
suffering 17–18, 19
    desire to explain reason
        for 67
    of Job 66–7
sympathetic nervous system
    181
symptom replication 161–2

TENS (Transcutaneous Electrical
    Nerve Stimulation) 59
thermal nociceptors 44
tinnitus 163
Tomlin, Lilly 56–7
top-down processing by the
    brain 93, 112
Transcutaneous Electrical Nerve
    Stimulation (TENS) 59
transduction 47
Travell, Janet 156–7, 158–9,
    171–2
    see also her entry in the author
        index
trigeminal nucleus caudalis 182
trigger points, myofascial
    autonomic sensations from
        163
    definition 155
    and fibromyalgia 183–4,
        184
    and headaches 168–9
    and heart attack symptoms
        166–7
    history of 156–9
    and labial pain 167–8
    as mimics 165–9
    and motor inhibition 164–5
    and nerve root compression
        173
    and overload 172–3
    potential causes 172–4
    and referred pain/sensation
        157–8, 162–5
    and replication of symptoms
        161–2

sensitivity 160
and shortened position 173
and testicular pain 167, 168
treatment non-availability
    174
trigger point complex 159
and the twitch response
    160–61
twitch response 160–61

ulcers 199–200

Veladone-RX 138
Verbal Reporting Scale (VRS) of
    pain 34, 34, 35
Vermeil, Al 107
virtual reality exposure (VRE)
    116
visceral nociceptors 45–7
Visual Analog Scale (VAS) of
    pain 34–5, 35, 38
visual components of pain
    112–13
visual processing 84–5
VRE (virtual reality exposure)
    116

walking speed, with back pain
    119–20
Wall, Patrick D. 40, 55, 59,
    124–5
Warren, J. Robin 199
weakness 164–5, 174
Weiss, Jay 133
whiplash 77, 183
wind-up 54–5, 185

ZIP 116

AUTHOR INDEX

Names in the index include research team members who may not actually appear by name in the text.

Ackerman, J. 200
Akerman, B. 115
Alarcon, R.D. 116
Alkalay, D. 183
Ariely, D. 137–138
Aro, T. 122
Aron, A. 191, 192

Banich, M.T. 117
Bantick, S. 96–97
Barr, J.S. 129
Begley, S. 99
Bennett, R.M. 176
Bennett, S.M. 41
Berns, G. 91
Bichot, N.P. 84–85
Blakeslee, S. 152
Blaser, M. 200
Bloom, J.R., 196
Bourne, P.G. 133–134
Brant-Zawadzki, M. 129
Bromley, L.M. 63
Brunet, A. 115, 116
Buskila, D. 183

Cabeza, R. 113–114
Cammilleri, S. 183
Carmon, Z. 138
Carrino, j. 128
Cekic, M. 91
Centeno, C. 61–62
Chabris, C. 83
Chambers, C.T. 41
Chang, L. 180
Chappelow, J. 91
Chatterjee, N. 191, 192
Cherin, E. 140
Chou, R. 128
Clare, S. 96–97
Clauw, D. 178
Colletti, R. 37
Corrigan, E. 112
Craig, K.D. 41
Curran, T. 117

De Simone, L.L. 39
Decety, J. 193
Depue, B.E. 117
Desimone, R. 84–85

Deyo, R. 122, 128
Di Pellegrino, G. 193
Dick-Read, G. 40–41
Diehl, A.K. 122
Diem, G. 140
Doenlen, R. 140
Dolcos, F. 113–114
Dufton, L.M. 37
Dupont, P. 183
Dyer, E.C. 105–106

Einarsson, E. 109
Eisenberger, N.I. 189, 190, 191
Engler, H. 140
Evans, S. 41

Fadiga, L. 193
Fan, C. 86, 88
Fields, H. 86, 88, 100, 101
FitzGerald, L. 180
Fogassi, L. 193
Freeman, M.D. 61–62
Friedlander, E. 143
Fu, R. 128
Furst, A. 86, 88

Gallese, V. 193
Gilovitch, T. 70
Giraux, P. 152
Goebel, M.U. 141
Goldman, D. 120
Gottheil, E. 196
Graap, K. 116
Gracely, R. 178
Grant, J.A. 95
Gruenewald, T.L. 39
Guedj, E. 183
Gurung, R.A.R. 39

Häkkinen, U. 122
Hanakawa, T. 86, 137
Harris, R. 178
Heft, R. 38
Heinrichs, T. 122
Hengge, U.R. 141
Hodges, L.F. 116
Hodges, P. 121
Honda, M. 86, 137

Inglis, B. 86, 88

Jackson, P.L. 193
Jarcho, J.M. 190
Jenkins, W. 99

Jensen, M. 129
Juhan, D. 66

Kajino, G. 130–131
Kaptchuk, T.J. 143
Katz, R. 181
Kelley, J.M. 143
Keltner, J. 86, 88
Klein, L.C. 39
Kluivers, K. 134
Kolata, G. 100
Konik, B. 37
Kou, W. 141
Kraemer, H.C. 196
Kshiguro, N. 130–131

LaBar, K. 113–114
Laine, C. 120
Lawndy, S. 134
Leavitt, F. 181
Levine, F.M. 39
Levine, P. 123
Lewis, B.P. 39
Lieberman, M.D. 189, 190, 191
Lurie, J.D. 130

Mackey, S. 191, 192
MacLean, P.D. 81
Malkasian, D. 129
Malmivaara, A. 122
Martin-Skurski, M. 91
Mason, J.W. 133–134
Master, S.L. 191
Masui, T. 130–131
Matsubara, Y. 130–131
Mayer, E.A. 180
McGill, S. 119
McLean, S., 178
McRae, C. 140
Meltzoff, A.N. 193
Melzack, R. 59
Menke, T.J. 139
Merzenich, M.M. 99–100
Meykadeh, N. 141
Milner, P. 142
Minton, K. 94, 123
Mixter, W.J. 129
Modic, M. 129
Moldofsky, H. 180
Moseley, J.B. 139
Myers, C. 38

Nader, K. 109, 115
Nakamura, S. 130–131

223

Naliboff, B. 180, 190–191
Neumann, L. 183
Niboyet, J., 183
Niemi, M.-B. 140
Nystrom, A. 61–62

Obuchowski, N. 129
Ogden, P. 94, 123
Okada, T. 86, 137
Olds, J. 142
O'Malley, K. 139

Pacheco-López, G. 140
Pagnoni, G. 91
Pain, C. 94, 123
Parke, S. 191, 192
Payne, K.B. 112
Petersen, N.J. 139
Ploghaus, A. 96–97
Price, D. 38

Rainville, P. 95
Ramachandran, V.S. 152
Ready, D. 116
Recanzone, G. H. 99–100
Redfern, R. 86, 88
Richmond, C.E. 63
Riether, C. 140
Rizzolatti, G. 193
Robinson, G.E. 105–106
Robinson, M. 38
Rose, R.M. 133–134
Rosenthal, M. 122
Ross, J. 129
Rossi, A.F. 84–85
Rothbaum, B. 116

Sanchez, M.N. 143
Sapolsky, R. 126, 133, 187–
        188, 199–200
Sawamoto, N. 86, 137
Scaer, R. 77, 123
Schedlowski, M. 141
Schreiner, C.E. 99–100
Schwartz, J. 99
Scott, D., 178
Shirinyan, D. 191
Shiv, B. 138
Sime, A. M. 134
Simons, D. 82–83
Simons, D.G. 155, 159
Sirigu, A. 152
Smith, S. 96–97
Smythe, H.A. 176
Spiegel, D. 196
Stains, J. 180
Stanger, C. 37
Staud, R. 184–185

Taylor, S.E. 39, 191
Tosteson, A.N.A. 130
Tosteson, T.D. 130

Tracey, I. 96–97
Travell, J.G. 155, 158–159
Tsao, J. 41
Tucker, K. 121

Updegraff, J.A. 39

Vaisberg, G. 183
Vierhout, M. 134

Waber, R.L. 138
Wall, P.D. 40, 55, 59
Weinstein, J.N. 130
Wickelgren, I. 40
Wilson, J. 120
Wise, E. 38
Wise, R. 96–97
Withagen, M. 134
Wolfe, F. 176, 183
Woolf, C.J. 55, 61, 63

Yamazaki, T.G. 140
Younger, J. 191, 192
Yukawa, Y. 130–131
Yunus, M.B., 176

Zeltzer, L.K. 41
Zink, C. 91
Zubieta, J.K. 178